TIME AND TIME AGAIN

First presented by Michael Codron on 16th August 1972 at the Comedy Theatre, London, with the following cast of characters:

Graham	Michael Robbins
Anna *his wife*	Bridget Turner
Leonard *her brother*	Tom Courtenay
Joan	Cheryl Kennedy
Peter *her fiancé*	Barry Andrews

The play directed by Eric Thompson
Setting by Alan Tagg

The action passes in Graham and Anna's conservatory, back garden and part of the recreation field

ACT I

   Scene 1   Spring

   Scene 2   A few weeks later

ACT II

   Scene 1   Autumn

   Scene 2   The following day

Time – the present

ACT I

SCENE 1

A suburban garden. Spring, a sunny, not particularly warm day

The garden is of the type that is separated, on either side, by fences which conceal other identical suburban gardens. This particular one has a scrap of lawn upon which stands an unattended, ancient lawn-mower. There is also a murky pond, over which presides a battered stone gnome. At one end of the garden we see part of the back of the Victorian terrace house to which it belongs. One of those glass boxed conservatories, obviously a later attachment to the original outside wall of the house. Through the windows we see garden furniture, tables and chairs, potted plants all in various stages of decay, some hanging from on high, some sprouting from pots circling the floor. A stained glass door leads from this to the rest of the house. Nothing seems in very good repair. At the other end of the garden a small pile of breeze blocks lies just inside the boundary fence, one of those made with concrete posts with wires threaded through them. Beyond this is more grass, being the edge of the local recreation ground

When the CURTAIN rises, Leonard, a man in his late thirties, is discovered in the conservatory. He is a pale, alert, darting sort of man. He wears a dark suit and a black tie. He breathes on the window and looks out at the garden for a moment. He comes outside and stares at it again. After a moment he removes his jacket and drops it by the pond. Now in his shirt-sleeves and braces he goes to the mower and tries, ineffectually, to push it. He tries a second time, but the blades appear totally jammed. He crouches down to try to mend it

Graham, a man of forty, stockier, more solidly built, enters the conservatory. He holds a glass of Scotch, and the end of a cigar. He watches Leonard struggling for a moment, before coming out into the garden

Graham So, you're out here then.

Leonard ignores him

You don't waste much time, do you? (*He flicks the end of his cigar into the pond and goes to the pile of breeze blocks. Kicking them*) I should clear these while you're at it. Been stuck here since before Christmas. (*He pauses*) You don't believe in wasting time, do you?
Leonard (*looking up*) Eh?
Graham Straight back and on with it, that's your motto.
Leonard (*absorbed again*) What?

Graham I mean your mother hasn't been buried ten minutes and you're back here cutting the bloody grass.

Leonard I'm not drinking, anyway.

Graham What do you mean? I'm toasting her on her way, that's all. Seeing her off with a toast.

Leonard It's a funeral you've been to, you know, not a launching.

Graham What's the harm? She wasn't my mother. I wasn't her son. I was a damn fine son-in-law, though I say it myself, but I wasn't her son.

Leonard She'd have confirmed that.

Graham What the hell are you doing?

Leonard Writing my memoirs.

Graham You should have greased it last year when you'd finished with it. Thin layer of grease over all the working parts.

Leonard Thank you. I'll remember that.

Graham Otherwise when you come to use them next year they've jammed. Like that one.

Leonard Useful tip that.

Graham Yes.

Leonard Except I wasn't here last year.

Graham Nor you were. Just seems like it.

Leonard Yes.

Graham (*suddenly jovial*) Tell you what, I'll nip upstairs and throw you the nail scissors out of the bathroom window. Cut the grass with those. Be quicker in the long run. With the nail scissors. Like they did in the army. Did you have that? Fatigues. We had this sergeant-major. One of his favourite little games that—cutting the grass with nail scissors. My God! We had some laughs in those days. Did you ever do that?

Leonard Not in the navy.

Graham Ah.

Leonard We used to paint it blue, instead.

Graham Blue?

Leonard The grass. It was a secret Admiralty device to run the enemy aground.

Graham (*puzzled*) I never heard of them doing that.

Leonard It was just an experiment.

Graham (*shaking his head*) I never heard of that.

Leonard They had to abandon it eventually. It confused the R.A.F. When they flew over it, they weren't sure which way up they were. Half bomber command were flying upside down at one time.

Graham I don't believe that for a minute. You're making the whole thing up. That's a pack of lies.

Leonard That's just what the Air Ministry said.

Graham I came out to have a word with you. Now then, I've invited young Peter back to tea.

Leonard How nice.

Graham I'll remind you he took care of a lot of the arrangements for your mother's funeral. Arrangements one might have hoped, others could have dealt with themselves. So, as a small way of saying thanks I've invited Peter and his girl to tea.

Leonard Good to see you keeping up relations with your employees.

A dog barks in the distance

Graham Oh, yes, I've got plans for young Peter, don't you worry. A very bright young man, that. He'll get on in this world. He's got a style about him. And a very presentable young fiancée, too. You see her? Very nice. Don't blame him, keeping her hidden away all this time ... (*He leers*)

Leonard You fancy her, then?

Graham The point I'm making is this. If you intend to grace us with your presence at teatime, may I remind you they have not come to hear the story of your life ...

Leonard You amaze me.

Graham Maybe I do. But I don't want a repetition of last Friday. When George Walker was here to dinner with his wife. All that embarrassing scene ...

Leonard What was that?

Graham All that argument about—sexual incompatibility and so on ...

Leonard Oh. I thought that livened things up a bit.

Graham Oh yes, fascinating. By the time we got to the flan you'd practically broken up their marriage. Her in floods of tears and him with his blood pressure at boiling point ... I'll have you know he's one of my most important clients.

Leonard I'm sorry. I thought that all went rather well.

Graham Well, it damn well didn't. It's cost me a fortune in drinks ever since. Just don't trail your failure through my house like—a pair of muddy boots.

Leonard That's awfully poetic. Please wipe your soul.

Graham And that's another thing. We don't want another of your damn poetry recitals either. You know your trouble?

Leonard (*who has been looking out over the recreation field*) Ah, they're taking up the goal-posts.

Graham Where?

Leonard Over there. Removing the goal-posts ...

Graham Oh yes. You know what your trouble is? (*He tinkers with the lawn-mower*)

Leonard Probably has tremendous local significance. Some primitive, suburban, spring fertility dance, no doubt. First, four little men, symbolically dressed in blue overalls—symbolic of what, I don't know ... Never mind. Men in symbolic blue overalls spill on to the field from their grey truck to perform the Annual Uprooting the Goal-Posts Ritual. The significance of the goal-posts is perfectly clear, of course. Two male uprights thrusting from the borough council's green soil to support, at each end, the dormant horizontal female crossbar. Soon to be awakened from her winter slumbers by the rough hands of the Parks Department employees ...

Graham You need a spanner on this. Get the blades off ...

Leonard And down she comes . . .

Graham Rusted in, this has.

Leonard Go careful with her, men! In her, rest all the parish's hopes of fertility . . . "Spring, the sweet Spring, is the year's pleasant king: Then blooms each thing, then maids dance in a ring . . ."

Joan, a woman in her early twenties, enters the conservatory with a tray of tea things and starts unloading them on the table

Graham What are you on about now?

Leonard I sing in praise of all women and the fruit that they will bear . . . (*Seeing Joan through the window*) Good gracious. Talk of the devil . . .

Graham Here, now listen. Don't you start on about all that stuff again. Just as we're going to have tea. I warned you.

Leonard (*back to the recreation field*) Whoops! He nearly dropped her on his head. That would have added a new dimension to the ceremony. "Acolyte coshed by earth mother . . ."

Graham Hey. If you're making some sort of snide references to me and Anna with all this talk of fertility and so on . . .

Leonard What?

Graham The doctor told her it would be injurious to her health. That's the only reason we haven't had any children. Not that it's any of your business.

The dog barks again, nearer

I'm as—as the next man. You can't talk. You've had three and look where that got you . . .

Leonard Here.

Graham Quite. Remember that.

Anna, in her late thirties, enters the conservatory with teapot and milk jug

Leonard Come on, lads!

The dog barks again, very close

Get stuck in, there!

Graham I don't think that's fitting behaviour in your funeral suit.

Leonard Why not? It's my suit for all seasons. Wedding, divorce, Coronation, Trooping the Colour—Mother said I was christened in it.

Joan exits with her tray

Anna (*calling*) Graham! Leonard! (*She closes the door, sits and pours tea*)

Graham Ah! Sounds like tea. Are you coming in and behaving properly?

Leonard I don't think I could honestly trust myself. I'd better have it out here . . .

Graham It's freezing cold . . .

Leonard With Bernard.

Graham Bernard? Who the hell's Bernard?
Leonard (*indicating the gnome*) Bernard.
Graham Oh, my God!
Leonard The last of the great coarse-fishing gnomes.
Graham Come on, Leonard. For heaven's sake. You can't sit out here.
They'll think something's the matter with you.
Leonard Tell them I'm meditating. You can't have it both ways. Either I
come in there and embarrass you or I stay out here and embarrass you.
Graham I just wish to hell you'd go . . .
Leonard Then I could ring you up and embarrass you.
Graham Look. I'll remind you that as from last Wednesday, this house
no longer belongs to your mother, you know. It belongs to me. Me.
You remember that.
Leonard Oh. I thought it belonged to your wife, somehow.
Graham All right. But if I decide to sling you out, she's not going to
argue with me, I can tell you that . . . (*He moves away to the conservatory*)

Conservatory wall slides away (*see Ground Plan*)

Joan enters the conservatory with five tea plates

Joan These are the ones, aren't they?
Anna Oh, thank you, Joan. It's just in case anyone wants a biscuit, that's
all. I hope no-one's too hungry.
Joan You can't do any more, not today. Nobody expects it.

Graham comes inside, closes the door and puts his glass down on the chest

Graham (*jovially*) Ah! Ha!
Anna Isn't Leonard coming?
Graham No, his Lordship prefers to have his tea out there, for some reason.
Joan Oh.
Anna Out there? But it's freezing out. And he's got his jacket off. Look at
him, he'll catch cold. Leonard! Leonard!

Leonard turns

(*Mouthing and miming*) Put your jacket on. Jacket—on . . .

Leonard beams at her, waves and turns away

Oh, he can't hear me. Graham, give him a call.
Graham Anna, he is not a child. If he wants to stay out there and freeze
in his shirt-sleeves . . .
Anna And you know who'll finish up nursing him.
Graham Yes, well . . . (*To Joan*) Joan, your Peter not here yet?
Joan No. I think he must still be at the garage.
Anna Awful that was for you. Breaking down in the cemetery car park.
All those hearses queued up behind you . . .
Joan Yes, it was rather . . . Thank you very much by the way, Mr Baker,
for—well, for letting me . . .
Graham Intrude on our grief. Not at all, you're welcome.

Joan It was just that, with me arriving only last night and then Peter having arranged to come to this today . . .

Anna It was only natural you'd both want to be together. We quite under-stand. Have you got somewhere to stay?

Joan Yes, I'm with Mrs Henderson.

Graham Oh.

Anna Oh, Mrs Henderson. (*On reflection*) Do I know her?

Joan She's a friend of Peter's mother.

Graham Ah . . .

Anna Oh, that's nice.

Joan Just round the corner.

Graham Ah . . .

Anna Lovely. You'd have liked our mother, Joan. She was a wonderful old lady . . .

Graham Yes indeed . . . (*A respectful pause*) You have brought a ray of sunshine, Joan, into an otherwise grey day . . .

Joan Thank you. I just hoped I hadn't upset your brother. I mean my coming round at this time . . .

Anna and Graham laugh

Anna Oh, no . . .

Graham There's not much that upsets Leonard. Don't you worry about that. What's he looking at out there, anyway?

Anna What's he looking at out there, anyway?

Graham Some men doing something with goal-posts. God knows. He's getting worse. He's getting steadily worse.

Joan Worse? How do you mean?

Graham Worse. Nutty. Off his head.

Anna Oh, Graham, really.

Graham Listen, I've been out there talking to him for ten minutes . . .

Anna Oh, no. Now he's sitting on that damp grass. (*Vainly calling*) Leonard! Leonard!

Graham Ten minutes I've been out there with him. I haven't understood three words he said.

Anna Now what's he been saying to you?

Graham I don't know. That's what I'm saying. I don't know what he was saying. Don't ask me. I mean, Joan, it's got so that you say one simple, straightforward sentence to the man and he's away. Raving. Off his head. We watched him one day, Anna and me, from the bathroom window up there, didn't we, Anna? Didn't we?

Anna Oh, now, Graham, be fair . . .

Graham I am being fair, Anna. I am being perfectly fair. The fact still remains—is it or is it not true, correct me if I'm wrong, we watched him for ten minutes from that bathroom window, standing in that garden, talking to that gnome. Anna was with me. I found out something else today, too. He calls him Bernard. Did you know that, Anna?

Anna Oh. He had a friend called Bernard when he was little.

Graham What, a school friend?

Anna No. He was invisible. One of those sort of friends. You know.

Graham Did you hear that, Joan? Did you hear that? This is his own sister saying this.

Joan Oh, I had one of those sort of friends. Called Mary. We always used to have to lay an extra place for Mary. She went away eventually and joined the Wrens. That's what I always wanted to be, you see.

Graham God love us. We've got another one of them here.

Anna Oh go on, Graham, every child goes through that. Don't tell me you didn't have an invisible friend?

Graham I certainly did not.

Joan Oh, what a shame.

Anna Actually, I don't think my husband ever was a child, Joan.

Graham If my father had ever caught me talking to invisible friends . . .

Anna His parents found him in a cupboard, aged eighteen . . .

Graham My father would have had his belt off to me. Six foot four, that man, Joan.

Anna Oh don't, dear.

Graham I'm just telling Joan. She'll be interested in this. Six foot four that man, Joan. And never had a day's illness in his life. And—you'll never believe this—the day that he was born . . .

Anna The doctors gave him a week to live.

Graham A week to live.

Joan That's amazing.

Anna Oh, not all that much. He was an awful old man with loose teeth who kept telling you he was living on borrowed time.

Graham Yes, well, so he was, so he was.

Anna He'd managed to borrow seventy-three years, by the time he died. He hadn't much to complain about. And he wasn't at all pleasant to your mother.

Graham The point I am making is that grown men do not stand around in gardens, talking to stone gnomes.

Anna Quite right, dear.

Graham Point taken?

Anna Yes.

Graham Good. Let's not talk about Leonard any more. What have we got to eat?

Anna Help yourself to biscuits. You know this house is going to be funny without mother.

Graham Biscuits? Is that all?

Anna I mean, it's always been her house, if you know what I mean, Joan. I know Graham and I have lived with her for five years, but I've never thought about it as my own home.

Graham I don't call biscuits much of a tea.

Anna Still, we won't be here for much longer. We're having this new bungalow built up at the back of the Fallowfield Estate. Do you know it at all. No, well, you wouldn't . . . Well, it's very picturesque up there. Yes, we were planning to take Mother up there with us when we moved, she'd have loved it. Anyway. Now I suppose we'll have to start sorting

out her things. She had so much you know, Joan. Old people are like
that, aren't they? They store things away. Just in case. For a rainy day.
Please God it won't be raining where she's gone.

Joan I'm sure it won't.

Graham If I'd known all we were getting was biscuits for tea, I'd have had
lunch.

Anna You had lunch.

Graham When did I have lunch?

Peter, a healthy-looking young man in his early thirties, enters

Peter Hallo. Sorry . . .

Graham (*jovially*) Ah ha! Ah ha!

Anna Oh, hallo, Peter. How's the car?

Peter I rolled it down the hill to the garage. Left it with them.

Graham Fan belt?

Peter Yes.

Graham Said it was, didn't I?

Anna Come and sit down, Peter. Have a cup of tea.

Peter Thank you, Mrs Baker.

Graham Always carry a spare fan belt. Good tip that. Save you a lot of
embarrassment.

Peter Sorry to mess up your funeral, Mr Baker.

Graham Wasn't my funeral. (*He laughs*)

Anna You couldn't help it, could you?

Graham Did you hear what I said? I said it wasn't my funeral.

Anna Yes, we heard you. Could have happened to anybody, that could.

Graham Personally, I always carry—a spare can of petrol, a spare fan
belt, spare wheel nuts . . .

Anna (*pouring tea for Peter*) You take milk, don't you?

Peter Thank you.

Graham Spare fuses. They're useful things.

Anna Sugar?

Peter Thank you, Mrs Baker.

Graham Spare water, spare bulbs . . .

Anna Help yourself, then, Peter.

Graham And finally, a flashlight. (*A pause. He repeats the list quietly to
himself, fearing he has missed something*) Yes.

Leonard goes and stands by the gnome, his back to the others

Joan It really is the most wonderful view you've got here, isn't it, darling?

Peter Oh, I love it. Always have. Right across the recreation field . . .

*They all look out. Leonard is chatting to Bernard, then, aware of their eyes
on him, turns and looks at them. They look away. Leonard goes and sits on
the breeze blocks*

You all right, darling?

Joan Fine, darling. Are you all right?

Peter Fine. Is that Leonard out there?

Anna Yes, it is. I suppose we ought to take him some tea.

Graham Hey. Just hold on a minute. When did I have lunch?

Anna What?

Graham You said I had lunch. When did I have lunch?

Anna At lunch-time.

Graham Well, it's the first I've heard of it.

Peter We had lunch.

Anna You had cold meat and salad.

Graham Oh, yes.

Peter We had roast beef.

Anna You had soup, cold meat and salad, cheese, half a packet of biscuits and coffee.

Graham Well, I don't call that a lunch. I call that a snack.

Anna All right, then. I'll make you some sandwiches.

Graham No, I'll have the biscuits. Don't bother.

Anna It's no bother. I'll cut some sandwiches.

Graham I've said. I'll have the biscuits.

Anna No, I'd rather.

Graham These are fine.

Anna Won't be a moment.

Graham Anna, please don't go rushing away from the table . . .

Joan I could make them . . .

Graham For heaven's sake sit down.

Anna No, I'll make them, Joan.

Peter Not for me. We had lunch.

Graham Well, I don't want them.

Anna I'm making them now, it's too late.

Joan Please let me do it . . .

Anna Joan, will you sit down.

Graham I shan't eat them.

Anna If I go to all the trouble to make sandwiches, you will damn well eat them.

Anna goes out

Graham Won't take no for an answer. That's her trouble. (*Yelling after Anna*) Not cheese. (*Appealing to the other two*) Still, I expect we'll all be glad of a sandwich.

Peter Not for us.

Joan No.

Peter We had lunch.

Graham That's more than we did. Well, now, Peter, where have you been hiding this one away, eh? (*Broadly winking*) I must say I prefer her to all the other girls you've brought round here. Eh? Eh?

Joan and Peter laugh half-heartedly

You ought to feed her up though, you know, Peter.

Peter What?

Graham Well, look at her. She's wasting away. There won't be enough left of her to marry, if you're not careful.

Joan What are you talking about? I've put on weight.

Peter Yes. I think she has a little.

Joan Not that much, though.

Peter No. Not that much.

Graham Well, I dread to think what she was like before. That's all. I mean look at these arms of hers. (*Grabbing her*) Look at this. Like a stick.

Joan (*pulling away*) Ouch!

Graham Like a stick. He wants something he can get hold of, girl. You ought to get her to take up one of those sports of yours, Peter.

Joan No, thank you.

Graham Come on. Good game of football. Do you good. He's tried to get me on that, haven't you?

Peter I've given that up, Mr Baker.

Graham No, the man you wanted on that football field, was my father. He'd have given you a game. Six feet four, fourteen stone, wonderful head of hair.

Peter I didn't know he was a sportsman.

Graham He wasn't. He had heart trouble. The whole of his life. Since birth. They gave him a week to live at one stage.

Peter Yes. I know. Did you know that, darling?

Joan Yes.

Graham Mind you, he felt all right. Never had a day's illness. He was fine. But he couldn't take risks. Not after a warning like that. Big hands, he had. Never seen hands like them on a man. He could have lifted you up, Joan, with one hand. That's if he'd dared risk it. Did I ever tell you . . . ?

Joan Excuse me, Mr Baker, but before you go on, do you think your brother-in-law would like a cup of tea?

Graham Probably. Let him come and get it if he does.

Peter What's he doing?

Graham God knows.

Joan I think I might as well take him some.

Graham Leave him alone.

Peter I'll take it to him, darling.

Joan No, I'll take it, darling, please. (*She pours a cup of tea*)

Peter No, let me, darling. It's chilly out there.

Joan (*reluctantly*) All right.

Graham If he can't be bothered to come in and get his own tea . . .

Joan Perhaps he's upset.

Graham Upset? Why?

Joan Well, with the funeral. His mother. People sometimes are, you know.

Graham Leonard? Upset? That'll be the day.

Joan (*giving Peter the cup*) Here you are, darling.

Graham That will be the day.
Joan Does he take sugar?
Graham God knows. He can never make up his mind.
Peter I think he does. I'll take some in the saucer.
Joan I'll hold the door.
Graham What a lot of fuss. Young man, if you leave me alone with her too long, I'm warning you I won't be answerable . . .
Joan (*as Peter goes outside*) Don't spill it, darling. (*She closes the door*)

Peter goes down the garden to Leonard

Graham No, you don't want to worry about my brother-in-law.
Joan Why not?
Graham He doesn't worry about anyone else.
Joan You're not very nice about him, are you?
Graham Huh!
Peter (*with Leonard*) Brought some tea for you, Leonard.
Leonard Oh. Thank you.
Peter Sugar's in the saucer.
Leonard Thanks.

There is a long pause between them. Leonard sips the tea and continues to stare. Peter hovers for a moment, then sits beside him on the mower

Graham You know what he used to do? He used to hide in cupboards and jump out at his mother when she came past.
Joan This was when he was little?
Graham Good God, no! Right up to a fortnight ago till she was taken ill.
Joan Did she mind?
Graham What?
Joan Him jumping out at her?
Graham No, she used to laugh her head off. She was as batty as he is. Do you know, she even tried to leave him this house. Till I talked her out of it. No wonder the father left them . . .
Joan Did he?
Graham Went for a walk to the corner, as far as the tobacconists. They never saw him again.
Joan There's a lot of cases of that happening, aren't there?
Graham Yes, why do you think they say smoking's bad for you? Eh? (*He laughs and nudges her*)
Joan More tea?
Graham Oh, seeing as you're mother . . . (*He holds out his cup*)
Peter Bit nippy out.
Leonard Very.
Graham I didn't mean that personally just now, by the way.
Joan What was that?
Graham About you being too thin. I hope you didn't take it personally.
Joan Oh.
Graham I always have a laugh with Peter. He likes me to pull his leg. I mean, I don't mind saying . . . He's a very lucky bloke. I mean, there's

no point in mincing words. You're a very attractive girl—I mean, what's
the point of beating about the bush—eh?

Joan I wouldn't know. Here. (*She passes him the cup*)

Graham Ta!

Peter Went off all right, I thought.

Leonard What's that?

Peter The funeral. I thought it went rather well.

Leonard Glad you enjoyed it.

Peter (*slightly alarmed*) I didn't mean that.

Leonard Ah.

Graham (*reaching out and patting Joan's leg just above the knee*) Some men
have all the luck, eh? Some men have it all . . . (*His hand lingers*)

Peter Perhaps I shouldn't have mentioned the funeral. You want to forget
about it.

Leonard Mmmm? No, I wasn't thinking about that.

Peter Oh.

Graham Some men have the luck of the devil.

Joan (*calmly*) Don't . . .

Graham (*playful*) Why not? Give me one good reason. Go on.

Joan Your brother-in-law is watching.

Graham He won't say anything. (*He takes a bite from his biscuit*)

Peter What were you thinking about?

Leonard I was thinking that my sister's husband's hand is at present resting
on your fiancée's thigh.

Peter (*turning*) What?

Graham snatches his hand away

Joan I told you.

Peter What was he doing?

Graham (*rising*) I'd better just go and see how those sandwiches are getting
on; I'll be back in a minute.

Graham goes into the house

Peter Mr Baker wasn't really doing that, was he?

Leonard Not really. Probably just a trick of the light. Anyway, his heart
couldn't have been in it.

Peter How do you mean?

Leonard He was eating a biscuit with the other hand.

Peter (*mouthing to Joan*) All right, darling?

Joan (*mouthing back*) Fine, darling.

Peter Anyway. I never have to worry about Joan.

Leonard No?

Peter Oh, no. We have complete trust. We've been separated a lot but
we've always had complete trust.

Leonard Is that a fact?

Peter Absolutely. We have to, you see. Because basically we're violently
jealous people. I mean if I so much as caught her looking at another man

—or more important—another man looking at her—(*he shakes his head*)—and vice versa . . . Funny, the only time we ever had any trouble was practically the first time we went out together. This was, oh—three years ago now. You see, I'd invited Joan out and then this other fellow thought he'd invited her out, too. And she didn't know who to choose. Deadlock. We had to go three rounds . . .

Leonard You and Joan . . . ?

Peter No. Me and this other fellow. You know—boxing. On with the gloves, into the ring. Well, I say that. It wasn't really as drastic as it sounds. We both used to train at this same gymnasium, anyway, you see. So off we went. Three three-minute rounds, a good clean fight and the best man won.

Leonard Who was that?

Peter Me.

Leonard Oh. Very romantic.

Peter I suppose it was, really.

Leonard And traditional. Fighting over a woman you love.

Peter And it's still a very good way to settle these things. No ill feeling afterwards, you see. We shook hands at the end of the fight and that was it. Didn't carry the grudge further than the ring.

Leonard What happened to the other fellow.

Peter Can't remember. Went abroad. Zambia, I think.

Leonard Zambia?

Peter Joined the police force or something. He was a very good boxer, I know that. Thank God for my reach. I nailed him with my reach, you see. (*Extending an arm*) Look at that. You see? I've got a pretty fair reach . . .

Leonard (*sparring with Peter; casually*) Pretty good. Mind you, if settling things that way became a common practice, the only men who'd ever get the girls—would be the ones with long arms—not the usual dimension a woman looks for in a lover . . .

Peter I mean, you could be a very short man. Then you could get underneath his reach and work on him from the inside, you see. Body punches . . .

Leonard (*dropping to his haunches*) Well, that opens up the ladies' choice to include dwarves and midgets, I suppose. It could mean the end of civilized man as we know him . . .

Peter No, no, I don't think you quite follow . . .

Leonard You're all right, anyway. As long as you keep your eyes open for sensual-looking midgets—like Bernard, there . . .

Peter (*glancing away*) Bernard?

Leonard lands a blow in Peter's stomach

Uh!

Leonard Sorry. (*He gets up*) Bernard. Our stone friend, there.

Peter Oh, yes. Is this your mower?

Leonard I think it came with the garden.

Peter It's jammed.

Leonard Yes.

Peter (*starting to tinker with the mower*) You're pretty fit. Still can't persuade you to turn out on the cricket field, can I?

Leonard No.

Peter You didn't teach games at school?

Leonard No. I taught English, History, Religious Instruction with a strong
bias towards the Old Testament and I had a rather attractive line in
Nature Walks . . .

Leonard and Joan exchange a look

Peter No sport at all.

Leonard I played croquet, once . . .

Peter Ah! Were you any good?

Leonard No. Perhaps I should have said—I once played croquet, once.
With my ex-headmaster and his wife who seemed to do little else. I
remember I smashed her ornamental bird table with my backswing.

Peter Pity I can't persuade you to play cricket, though. You live practically
on the field. All you've got to do is jump over that fence . . .

Leonard That's the bit that deters me.

Peter The Occasionals are going to be pretty short of men this year.

Leonard The who?

Peter The East Pendon Occasionals. That's what we call ourselves. You've
probably seen our fixture list. It's on that board on the left-hand side
just as you're going into the reading room of the public library.

Leonard Really?

Peter That's us.

Leonard Oh, those East Pendon Occasionals. Terrific.

Peter I can put your name down?

Leonard No.

Peter Oh.

Leonard I think not. I'll just practise leaping the fence this year.

Joan comes out into the garden

Joan Aren't you two getting cold out here? Hallo.

Leonard Hallo.

Peter (*starting to get up*) Oh hallo, darling, we were just—aaaaahhh!

Joan What's the matter?

Peter I think I've got my fingers jammed in the blades.

Joan Oh God!

Leonard Hang on. (*He takes hold of the handles*)

Peter Aaaaahhh!

Joan Keep still, darling, keep still . . .

Leonard Hold on. I'll roll it back. Release the blades.

Peter Aaaaa!

Joan Hold on, darling.

Leonard Let me know if this is better . . . (*He pulls the mower gently back-
wards*)

Peter Yes—yes—no—other way—*other way!*

Joan (*screaming*) Other way!

Leonard Sorry. Other way.

Peter (*pulling his fingers clear*) Aaaaah.

Joan Let me see, darling . . .

Peter (*pulling away from her*) No. It's all right. All right.

Joan Is it bleeding?

Peter No, no. Hardly at all. I'm fine. (*He backs away to the conservatory door*)

Joan Well, let me wash it for you, darling.

Peter No, darling, please. (*Backing into the conservatory*) I'll do it. You stay there.

Graham enters from the house with a plate of sandwiches. He is followed by Anna

Graham What's up with you?

Peter (*pushing past them*) Nothing. Nothing. Just a scratch.

Peter goes into the house

Anna What happened?

Leonard Caught his fingers in the mower.

Graham (*suspiciously*) Oh, yes?

Anna I'd better see to him. Oh dear.

Anna exits

Graham Nasty that. Fingers in the mower. Happened to me once.

Joan Oh, really?

Leonard (*to Joan, quietly*) Practically everything's happened to Graham, you know. He's lived an amazingly full life . . .

Graham What's he on about?

Leonard Nothing.

Graham I bet. (*Holding up his plate, for Joan's benefit*) Got my sandwiches.

Joan Good.

Graham What do you think she's given me? Cheese. You heard me ask her, didn't you? Cheese. I'm shutting this door. It's letting the heat out. You coming in?

Joan In a minute.

Graham (*reluctantly*) Well. I'm shutting this door.

Graham shuts the door and sits in the kitchen armchair with his sandwiches, watching them through the window

Leonard No, there's not much that hasn't happened to Graham, really. It's quite an experience, sitting watching the news on television with him. Riots, fires, erupting volcanoes, people falling off mountains—he always says the same thing. That happened to me once. I think he must get all my share of exciting things, as well. While he's getting all the fun of being struck by lightning or half eaten to death by soldier ants, here am I . . . Perhaps you'd be very nice and push me in the pond, just to start the ball rolling. No, better not. That'd upset Bernard. Have you met Bernard? According to your fiancé, women find him physically attractive. Does he appeal to you at all? He's very even tempered, a hundred and two years old and his hobbies are fishing and staring . . . What do you say?

Joan Are you talking to me?

Leonard (*looking round*) I think I must be.

Joan I don't think we've been introduced properly. I'm Joan. (*Holding out her hand*)

Leonard (*shaking her hand*) Leonard. How do you do?

Joan Your hands are freezing. Why don't you come indoors?

Leonard I'm the open-air type.

Joan You don't look it.

Leonard I'm usually out here weight-lifting at this time of day, only my vest is at the launderette.

Joan I thought Peter said you were a school-teacher.

Leonard No, I've temporarily retired from that. I'm at present plucking up courage to try something else . . .

Joan Have you got anything in mind?

Leonard Well, today I was rather attracted by the idea of driving a hearse. Nice quiet job, wonderful leisurely tempo. Long hours spent in peaceful cemetery car parks, having a respectful cigarette, waiting for the mourners to return—it looked attractive.

Joan I'd have thought you might have gone for something a bit more cheerful.

Leonard Ah, well, beggars can't be choosers, can they? "Too late for love, too late for joy, too late, too late! You loiter'd on the road too long, you trifled at the gate,"—er . . .

Joan What?

Leonard Christina Georgina Rossetti.

Joan Who?

Leonard A poem, that's all.

Joan Oh. Do you know poetry?

Leonard No. None at all. But I used to have to teach it. I devised an infallible system to fool all headmasters and school inspectors. I learnt the first two lines of every poem I could in the *Oxford Book of English Verse*. It made me sound terribly knowledgeable. Only the first two lines, mind you, nothing else. "She was a phantom of delight when first she gleam'd upon my sight": Wordsworth.

Joan You could always work for your brother-in-law.

Leonard I could. But I won't.

Joan Oh.

Leonard Are you going to?

Joan No.

Leonard Not even to be near Peter?

Joan No.

Leonard Good opportunities for a bright girl. A friendly hand on your thigh in times of stress.

Joan Yes, I thought you'd seen that.

Leonard I'm afraid I tried to make Peter jealous, but he wasn't having any.

Joan Peter only notices what he wants to.

Leonard But once he's roused . . .

Joan How do you mean?

Leonard He was telling me he once fought for your hand.

Joan When was this?

Leonard The first time he took you out.

Joan Did he? I don't remember that.

Leonard Oh, don't disappoint me. With a prospective Zambian policeman.

Joan Oh, you mean Mike. Well, they might have done. They used to have sparring matches in the gym every Thursday, anyway. I think they had some arrangement that whoever won could take me out on the Saturday.

Leonard Didn't you have any say, at all?

Joan I didn't mind, really. As long as one of them turned up . . .

Leonard No particular preference?

Joan Well, I suppose I sometimes hoped it would be Mike, because Mike had a car. But then Peter was a better dancer. It didn't really matter. It's like that when you're young, isn't it? Anyway, when Mike decided to emigrate, he sold Peter his car and that more or less decided it. Worked out rather well, really.

Leonard Yes. I think I preferred his version. (*He moves to the mower*) I'm not keeping you, am I? (*He pushes the mower*) It's jammed again. He must have left one of his fingers in it.

Joan Oh, don't. I ought to see if he's all right . . .

Leonard He looks the type who prefers to suffer alone.

Joan You're right there.

Leonard That's a sportsman's characteristic, that. No sympathy, please, but a round of applause when he comes back on the field. That's all he asks for.

Joan I suppose there are worse things than being a sportsman.

Leonard Oh, quite.

Joan I mean he could sit around doing nothing at all.

Leonard Yes. He could do. Perhaps he just never thought of it.

Joan Perhaps he did and decided it would be a bit pointless.

Leonard Perhaps. You're very attractive when you're cross. Did you know that?

Joan And I can do without those sort of . . . Oh, God!

Leonard What?

Joan Nothing.

Leonard What's the matter?

Joan Nothing. He's staring again, that's all.

Leonard Who, Graham?

Joan He was staring at me all through the church service, now he's staring at me again.

Leonard He stares at everyone. He's second only to Bernard.

Joan Peter said I was imagining it.

Leonard Does he bother you?

Joan Well, no—it just—yes, it does . . .

Leonard turns towards Graham, smiles and waves

Leonard Stop staring, you great bald-headed twit.

Joan (*alarmed*) Don't!

Graham, suspiciously, waves back

Leonard (*to Joan*) It's all right, he can't hear me. (*Shouting*) Can you, bun face! (*To Joan*) I did this once and found he had the window open. Is he still staring? Have a quick look.

Joan Yes. Eating his sandwiches and staring—right at me . . .

Leonard Do something rude.

Joan What?

Leonard Go on. Stick your tongue out at him. I dare you.

Joan I can't do that.

Leonard Why not?

Joan Well, apart from the fact that he's Peter's boss . . . You stick your tongue out.

Leonard He wouldn't believe his eyes if you did it. If I did it he would. Go on. He'll choke on his sandwich. Go on. I dare you.

Joan You're like a child, honestly. All right I will.

Joan sticks out her tongue at Graham. Graham chokes

(*Turning away*) Oh God!

Leonard What?

Joan (*overcome with laughter*) He choked on his sandwich.

Leonard joins in her laughter. He rolls on the grass

Anne enters with fresh-made tea and sees Graham

Anna Now what's the matter?

Graham Nothing. I'm just choking, aren't I? On this damn cheese . . .

Anna I don't know. There's Peter in the kitchen, you in here and . . . What's Leonard up to, now?

Graham He's your brother. Don't ask me.

Anna What can Joan be thinking? He just doesn't care. (*Opening the door*) Leonard! Goodness it's freezing out here. Leonard, dear, do come inside, both of you.

Leonard (*recovering slightly*) Right. You coming?

Joan Right. (*Wiping her eyes*) Oh, dear . . .

Leonard (*taking her hand*) You've gone all pink.

Joan Have I?

Leonard I think it's rather your colour . . .

Joan takes her hand away and they both go inside, Leonard closing the door

Anna (*pouring tea*) I've made some fresh tea. I hope Peter's all right, I left him out there.

Graham I would have thought Joan would be running to his side with bandages, if she were doing her stuff properly.

Joan He prefers to be left alone.

Graham That's a fine thing.

Anna I should say he does. He practically barged me into the rubbish bin when I tried to have a look.

Graham I hope he's washed that cut, that's all. You can get tetanus from a cut like that. Easiest thing in the world. Very nasty that.

Leonard You got over yours all right, though. (*He jabs Joan in the arm*)

Graham My what?

Leonard Tetanus.

Graham What tetanus?

Leonard Oh, I'm sorry, I thought you were going to tell us about the time you had tetanus.

Joan starts to giggle

Graham What are you talking about, now? I never said I'd had tetanus. When did I say a single word about me having tetanus?

Anna Do we have to talk about tetanus over tea?

Graham (*looking at Joan*) What's the matter with her?

Joan (*incapable*) Nothing.

Graham Is she crying, or something?

Anna You all right, dear? We're all on edge today. It's only natural.

Graham I'm not.

Peter enters

Anna Oh, Peter, how is it?

Peter Be all right. Nothing broken. I washed the cut, strapped it up. I'll have to leave you to do the driving, darling, I . . . You all right?

Joan Yes.

Peter Looking a bit flushed. You haven't stayed out there too long, have you?

Graham Been out there far too long, if you ask me. Talking to laughing boy here.

Leonard Me?

Anna Come and sit down, Peter.

Graham If there is one thing I can't stand it is people who laugh and snigger behind people's backs . . .

Leonard Yes, I know the sort of people you mean. Cinema usherettes, those sort of people, you mean?

Joan starts to giggle again

Graham You know damn well what I mean . . .

Anna Graham, really!

Graham No, I'm sorry, Anna. I've been giving him the benefit of the doubt far too long. Well, I'm saying this to you now, Leonard, and I'm saying it in front of witnesses—for Anna's sake, and for Anna's sake only—I am prepared to allow you to remain under this roof. But, come next winter, as soon as that new bungalow of ours is finished . . .

Leonard's laughter is beginning to infect the others. Even Peter is smiling in a slightly bewildered way

Anna I thought you said it wouldn't be . . .

Graham As soon as we've moved, you're on your own. Is that clear?

Anna He can have that little bedroom that was meant for mother.

Graham I'm not having him in there. I'll convert it to a bathroom.

Anna It's already got two. We'll have more bathrooms than bedrooms.

Graham No, I'm sorry I've put up with enough from him. Deliberately undermining my authority in my own house, under my own roof . . .

Anna Oh, shut up and drink your tea.

Graham I will not be undermined.

Leonard And that concludes the chairman's annual report to shareholders.

Graham I . . .

The others laugh

Anna You shut up, too, Leonard. You're as much to blame. You're always setting him off.

Leonard I'm sorry. I won't undermine him again.

Graham Yes, well, I should keep to that if I were you. I mean, I don't think someone in your position has much right to say anything, really. A man whose marriage finishes up with his wife locking him out of his own house hasn't really got a leg to stand on. Now that I consider funny. That's really funny, that is.

A silence

Anna Well, if you've both finished. Peter, would you like another cup of tea?

Peter Er—yes, thank you, Mrs Baker. (*With a furtive glance at his watch*) We mustn't be too long. Must we, darling?

Joan No—I told Mrs Henderson, I'd . . .

Anna Well, there's no need to rush away on our account. (*After a pause*) Oh, it is quiet without Mother, isn't it? Now then, Leonard. Where's your cup?

Leonard (*rising*) Oh. It's in the garden. I'll get it. (*Turning in the doorway*) By the way, Peter . . .

Peter Yes?

Leonard I think I'll say yes to that cricket invitation, after all.

Peter Oh. Great. Wonderful.

Leonard If you don't mind giving me a bit of practice . . .

Peter Sure.
Leonard (*going out*) Mind you. I suppose I'll pick it up as I go along.
Peter Yes.
Leonard Good.

Leonard closes the door. Peter wanders back to his chair and sits. Leonard has an imaginary bowl in the garden, and glares out over the playing field. Graham clears his throat. Joan turns to him. Aware of her eyes on him, Graham turns to her. She gives him a weak smile. Graham preens himself, as—

the CURTAIN *falls quickly*

SCENE 2

The same. It is now a hot day in June

Graham and Anna are seated in deck-chairs in the garden. She knits, while he stares out at the recreation field, where a cricket match is in progress. Joan lies out full length on the grass, sunbathing on her robe. From time to time the sound of cricket bat and ball is heard

Graham (*blowing his nose*) Sixty-three for seven. What a team! I ask you. The East Pendon Occasionals . . . You can't get more occasional than sixty-three for seven.
Anna They've got a lovely day for their game, anyway.
Graham Maybe they have. I don't think I can sit out here much longer. I'm telling you. (*He blows his nose again*)
Anna Is it bad?
Graham Streaming. It's all this damn grass. God knows what the pollen count is round here. It's that Leonard. He does it deliberately. Every time I decide to come out here to sit, he mows the damn grass.
Anna I don't think it's deliberate . . .
Graham (*yelling*) Oh, come on. Hit it, man. Hit it.
Anna Don't do that, dear.
Graham Dear, oh dear, oh dear. Looking at this lot, I think I should have offered to play. I couldn't do any worse, that's certain. He should have put that one away in the *Fox and Hounds* car park.
Joan They're not professionals, you know.
Graham You don't say. I'd never have guessed.
Anna Still, Leonard hasn't had a bat yet, has he?
Graham Oh, good gracious. I'd forgotten. We're saved, then, we're saved. We've got Mr Number Eleven to come. I bet you if I sneeze while he's taking guard, I'll have missed his innings. I saw them practising the other day. Peter bowling to him. The only ball that touched Leonard's bat, knocked it out of his hands. Not that Peter's much better. How many did he get? Three?

Joan Four.

Graham Beg his pardon. Four. The whole thing'll be over by tea-time. Mark my words . . .

Anna Yes, I'll put the kettle on in a minute. You'd like a cup, wouldn't you, Joan?

Joan Love one. Can I help?

Anna No, you stay there, dear. I'll do it.

Graham Don't you move. I'll rub your back in a minute, if you ask me nicely . . .

Joan I can manage, thank you.

Anna He never rubs my back . . .

Joan Leonard hasn't been in yet, has he?

Graham You'll hear the cheers when he is.

The sound of a bat and ball is heard, and applause

Anna Oh. I saw Mrs Carter this morning.

Graham Oh? Who's Mrs Carter?

Anna You know that woman who lives up at—over on—you know—always wears her hair in a bun—married to . . .

Graham Oh, her. What about her?

Anna Well, she said she passed our bungalow yesterday on her way to her osteopath. Said it was coming on beautifully . . .

Graham Well, she's got better eyesight than I have. That's all I can say. If those fellows laid three bricks last week, I'll be surprised. It'll need renovating before they've finished it, at this rate.

Anna (*packing away her knitting*) Well, she said it looked lovely from the road. It's not often we can sit out here, is it?

Graham (*sniffing*) I don't think I can much longer.

Anna Did you take those tablets?

Graham They're no good.

Anna Shall I fetch your drops?

Graham They're worse than useless.

Anna (*going on*) Suit yourself.

Anna exits

Graham (*regarding Joan*) If you lie there like that much longer, I shan't be responsible for . . . (*Sneezing*) Oh, God!

Joan You don't sound as if you'd make it.

Graham It's no bloody joke, this isn't.

Joan I'm sure.

Graham It's hereditary. My father had it. He was a big man too. Every time he sneezed it was like thunder. "God's in his heaven, again", my mother used to say. I hear you don't want to work for me.

Joan What?

Graham Young Peter tells me you'd prefer not to work with us.

Joan I think it's better.

Graham I could make you a damn sight better offer than what you're getting at the moment.
Joan I'm happy.
Graham Oh, well. I've offered. (*He touches her shoulder*) Here, you're drying up in this sun . . .
Joan I'm all right.
Graham (*touching her back*) You're red hot here. Your skin's beginning to burn . . .
Joan Oh, please!
Graham Here you are. I'll rub some oil in.
Joan (*irritated*) I don't want it . . .
Graham No, you need oil. Here. (*He slaps some oil on her back*)
Joan Ow!
Graham Lie still then. Lie still.
Joan (*sighing*) Oh, heavens . . .
Graham There. That's better, isn't it?

Joan grunts

Saw you walking along with Leonard, the other evening . . .
Joan Did you?
Graham Last Thursday evening. Passed you both in the car. You didn't see me. Very absorbed . . .
Joan Really? I think he was on his way back from cricket practice with Peter. I walked a bit of the way with him.
Graham Oh. That's nice.
Joan You could have given him a lift.
Graham I didn't like to interfere.
Joan Not everyone's like you, you know . . .
Graham Me? (*He stops oiling her*) What have I done?

Peter, in cricket flannels and a blazer, enters from the recreation field over the fence

Peter (*breathlessly*) Have you seen Leonard, by any chance?
Joan No.
Peter Can't seem to find him. He'll be in soon. Hope he hasn't wandered off somewhere . . .
Graham Four runs. Hah! What sort of a score do you call that?
Peter Bloke at this end's getting them to turn a bit. Had one came right back at me.
Graham Probably bounced off the cow parsley.
Peter Well, tell him I'm over by the changing hut, if you see him . . .
Graham If we see him. (*He pours more oil into his hand*)
Peter You all right, darling?
Joan Fine, darling!
Peter I wouldn't have too much of that oil, darling.
Graham She's drying out.
Peter Well, I think that's enough. It's not good to have too much.

Joan Yes. Thank you very much, Mr Baker.
Graham Always willing to oblige.
Peter See you, darling.
Joan Yes. 'Bye.

Peter goes, jumping over the fence

Graham Always comes along at the wrong moment. That's his trouble. (*Looking at the game*) Oh, just look at that. Fishing about outside his off stump like a great fairy queen . . . (*Yelling*) Hit it, you ninny! It's hot, isn't it?
Joan (*drowsy*) Mmmm.
Graham It reminds me of when we were first married, you know. We didn't have very much then, of course. If it was a week-end like this, I used to say to Anna—come on, then. We're off. And then we just used to drive. Terrible old car we had, too. Never sure how far we'd get in it. And never knew where we were going. Just drove and drove. Till we got hungry. Then we'd stop. Wherever we were. Put out the table. Have a picnic.
Joan What, in the road?
Graham No, not in the road. On the verge. On the grass verge. Marvellous picnics Anna used to make. Veal and ham pies. I remember we always had wonderful veal and ham pies.
Joan I always wondered who they were.
Graham Who?
Joan Those people who sit on the edge of main roads having tea. I always wondered who they were.
Graham That was us.
Joan I should have guessed. Wasn't it a bit dusty? Eating there?
Graham We were young, woman. A bit of dust doesn't hurt you. (*He sneezes*) I didn't have this then, mind you. Oh, I'll have to go in. It's no good. I'll have to go in.

There is the sound of bat and ball, and applause

Leonard comes out, with a cricket bat. He is also dressed for cricket, but his flannels are borrowed and ill-fitting. His blazer is a rather loud check sports coat and his shirt an ordinary white one unbuttoned at the neck and filled with a rather unsuitable cravat. The incongruous ensemble is rounded off with an "Occasionals" cricket cap. He walks awkwardly in his new, studded cricket boots

Bloomin' hell. What have you come as? Well, I've seen some . . . Peter's looking for you, you know. You ought to be getting your pads on. Only a couple more to go and you're in.
Leonard There's no hurry. I have to wait till someone else is out. Anyway, they've only got three pairs of pads.
Graham Roll on the Occasionals . . . (*He sneezes*)

Leonard Bless you.

Graham goes inside the house, muttering, and exits

How do you think I look? (*He leans on his bat*)

Joan Well—I don't want to be critical but . . .

Leonard You don't have to tell me. Why do you think I've been lurking upstairs all this time? I think I'll keep this jacket on when I bat.

Joan Is that usual?

Leonard Probably not, but neither are these trousers . . . I think they were made for someone like Graham's father, fourteen stone, six foot four, wonderful head of hair. At least this jacket does a little to conceal them. And I'm far too old to walk out there and have eleven fielders, two umpires and a batsman sniggering at me. Do you like my boots? They're made for a man with no toes. I suppose English cricketers, after years of wading across waterlogged wickets, must have developed webbed feet.

Joan laughs. Leonard sits and starts taking off his boots

I'm only doing this for you, you know. There's no need to laugh.

Joan What? Why for me?

Leonard It worked as well. I've seen a lot more of you than I would have done. I'm paying for it now, mind you.

Joan Are you all like this in this family?

Leonard What do you mean?

Joan Making sly sort of remarks . . .

Leonard What sly remarks?

Joan I can see more of you. All this business.

Leonard That's not sly.

Joan No?

Leonard Not at all. I'm in love with you, that's all.

Joan (*after a pause*) I think I'd better go and sit somewhere quieter.

Leonard I'm serious.

Joan (*offhand*) No, you're not.

Leonard Why should I say it then?

Joan I don't know. It's a sunny day, the pollen count is high, there's nobody else much around at the moment—I don't know. Your elegant flannels have gone to your head.

Leonard There's enough of them to, if I hitch them right up—so I take it you refuse to accept my statement?

Joan Totally.

Leonard In that case I shall bat without my jacket and I shall leave you to read off the verdict in due course. Death by Embarrassment . . .

There is the sound of bat and ball, and applause

Aha! Seventy-two for seven now. We're galloping on.

Joan Do you ever hear from your wife?

Leonard Mmm? My wife? No . . .

Joan Do you wish you did?

Leonard It wouldn't be proper, would it? She's a respectably married woman again, now.

Joan Do you miss your children?

Leonard Sometimes. (*He turns away and practises a stroke*)

Joan I'm sorry. That wasn't a very nice question.

Leonard No, not at all. At bath times, mainly, I miss them, I think. When I'm running a bath. Probably because that was one of the few things I ever did for them, run their bath. I couldn't take a bath for weeks after I'd left them. Really terribly anti-social . . .

Joan And she really locked you out?

Leonard In a way, I suppose she did. It was the evening I usually stayed on later at the school. The senior photographic society used to meet after hours. Not that I knew anything about photography, but the headmaster insisted a member of staff stayed behind to make sure the dark room was only put to the use intended. It was part of his campaign to reduce the student birth-rate. Anyway, between six and seven-thirty, every Thursday, I used to have to stand propping the dark room door open with my foot, letting light into their snapshots and keeping my eyes open for furtive coupling—in the words of the headmaster. However, on this particular day, the lights fused in the dark room—which sounds a bit paradoxical, but there you are—so I turfed them all out, locked up and came home early. And talking of furtive coupling . . .

Joan Your wife?

Leonard Yes. Not that I was surprised. I'd known about this chap for some time. I'd simply forgotten that he'd probably be there. They weren't in bed together or anything like that. They were sitting sampling his home-made wines, I seem to remember. Still, my arrival seemed to indicate to them that some sort of show-down was in order. I wasn't particularly keen to have one, but she'd gone to all the trouble of packing the children off to her mother's round the corner, so we settled down to an adult heart-to-heart . . .

Joan And then they locked you out?

Leonard No, I made a very dignified exit from the flat, got downstairs and found I'd forgotten my suitcase. Well, I rang and banged on the door and shouted, which everyone seemed to hear but them. I think they were afraid that I'd either turned homicidal or worse, I'd changed my mind and decided not to leave after all . . .

Joan So you just walked away? Just like that?

Leonard The police actually thought it was quite a joke.

Joan You went to the police then?

Leonard I had to sleep somewhere. I'd have gone to her mother's only I had a feeling she'd lock me out as well and I couldn't stick that twice in a night. The police were very nice, though. Thought it was the funniest thing they'd ever heard. And knowing what they had to cope with in that district, it probably was. This sergeant kept saying, "How did you get her to do it, you crafty devil. I wish I could persuade mine." I didn't get a wink of sleep. Every time a fresh batch of coppers arrived for duty, he had me telling them all over again. It was like a one-man police concert.

Joan Well. That's sad. I'm sorry.

Leonard That's all right. (*He smiles*)

Joan (*getting up suddenly*) Not the best technique, though, you know.

Leonard What?

Joan With women. Running yourself down, like you are. There are some who might feel sorry for you but there are a lot who just get turned off completely.

Leonard Really? Which sort are you?

Graham enters, and stops as he sees them

Joan (*stroking Leonard's cheek*) Guess.

Graham My God! Anna—Anna . . . !

Graham goes in to the rest of the house

Joan starts to climb through the fence

Peter enters from the recreation field

Peter Ah, Leonard, thank God. I thought you'd wandered off. (*Helping Joan*) Can you manage, darling?

Joan Thanks.

Peter Where are you going?

Joan Just a walk round the ground. I want some air.

Peter Oh, O.K. You all right, darling?

Joan Fine.

Joan exits

Peter What's wrong with her?

Leonard The heat.

Peter You think so? I bought her a sun hat the other day. She never wears it. Says it isn't flattering. I told her, it isn't to flatter you, it's to keep the sun off. (*He collapses in a deck-chair*) This is a hell of a stand these two are putting up—(*calculating*)—sixty—seventy-eight—that's twenty-five they've put on . . .

Anna enters the conservatory with Graham behind her

Graham(*pointing triumphantly*) There!

Anna What?

Graham (*looking*) She's gone.

Anna Is that it?

Graham What's he done with her?

Anna I left the kettle boiling . . .

The sound of bat and ball is heard

Peter Oh. Good shot . . .
Graham She was stroking his face.
Anna She may have been rubbing oil in. You're not the only one, you
know.

Anna goes back out

Graham lingers to cast one more suspicious look at Leonard

Graham I tell you, he's up to something. That man is up to something . . .

The sound of bat and ball is heard

Graham exits

Peter Oh, lovely! Perfect cover drive. (*He applauds*)

Leonard joins in vaguely

I didn't know Harry had those sort of shots in him. If this grass had been
shorter that would have been four all the way. That's the trouble with
this sort of cricket. You play good orthodox strokes you don't get anywhere.
Leonard Should suit my style admirably.
Peter Whoops! He didn't know much about that one. Don't forget you've
got your boots off, will you?
Leonard I couldn't.
Peter I'd like you to know I really do appreciate you turning out like this
for us. Giving up your Sunday. It was a very nice gesture.

There is the sound of bat and ball

Shot!
Leonard Not at all.
Peter I hadn't quite realized how—rusty you were, actually. You really
were pretty out of touch. Not that I'm worried you'll let us down or
anything. Don't think that. (*Watching the cricket again*) Steady, steady.
That was uppish. Len, do you mind if I ask your advice on something,
personal. I mean, I've really no business asking you—but I've come to
respect your opinion on things quite a bit . . .
Leonard (*surprised*) Really?
Peter It's to do with Joan . . .
Leonard Joan?
Peter And—Mr Baker. Your brother-in-law. I mean it sounds stupid but
you don't think he'd—try anything with her, do you? It's very awkward,
you see, with him being my boss and everything. He wants Joan to
work for him. But I told her I thought it was best if she didn't. Makes it
embarrassing. He does seem to hang around her a bit.
Leonard Well. I think it probably better that she doesn't work for him.
Peter You do?

Leonard I mean, good heavens, far be it for me to say a word against Graham . . .
Peter No, quite.
Leonard But. When a man gets to his age—well . . . (*He smiles*)
Peter Oh, yes . . .
Leonard Nothing to worry about. Bit sad in a way . . . So long as you keep an eye on him, now and again . . .
Peter Well, I don't really want to start . . .

A cry of "Howzat" is heard, and applause

Oh, he's bowled him—a yorker. You'd better get your boots on. You're in after next.
Leonard Yes. (*He gropes for his boots*)
Peter I don't reckon this next chap'll last long. He's got a torn ligament.
Leonard (*struggling*) I bet he's got boots that fit him, though.

Anna enters the conservatory with a tray of tea things which she puts on the table

Anna Would you like your tea out there or in here?
Peter Oh, thanks all the same, Mrs Baker. They lay on something for the players at the back of the hut . . .
Anna All right. Oh, doesn't Leonard look nice. Where's Joan?
Leonard These idiotic boots.
Anna Where's Joan?
Peter Over the far side. Walking round the ground.

Applause is heard

Anna She'll have a cup. Isn't that little man walking along with the hat, the manager of that supermarket on the corner?
Peter Wally Huggett. That's right. Played a damn good innings. (*He applauds*)
Anna I'll have a word with him later. He overcharged me last Tuesday.

Graham comes out from the house

Graham I saw that last wicket. From the bathroom window. Lovely ball. Bat and pad. (*To Leonard*) Hey! Shouldn't you be getting ready?

The sound of bat and ball is heard, then applause

Leonard (*through gritted teeth*) I am getting ready.
Graham Hey! He's hit that first one. A real sky-er.
Peter Good shot!
Graham He's going to be caught . . .
Peter No, it's cleared him.
Graham Never . . .
Peter It's past him.
Graham Straight down his throat . . .

Peter Oh, no!

Cheers are heard

Anna Is he out?
Graham He's out!
Peter (*to Leonard*) You're in.
Leonard Oh, God!
Peter Don't worry about the boots . . .
Leonard (*needled*) What do you mean? Don't worry about the boots? What do you want me to do? Go on bloody barefooted?

Peter helps Leonard on with his boots

Graham Leonard's in now, Anna!
Anna Oh, good . . .
Graham Providing they're all prepared to wait for him.

A slow handclap is heard

Peter (*kneeling by Leonard*) You can take over Denis's pads as he comes out . . .
Anna I was just saying, Graham, doesn't Leonard look nice?
Graham This bowler's on a hat trick now . . .

Joan enters from the field

Joan Is it Leonard they're all waiting for?
Peter (*flustered*) Of course it is, darling, why do you think we're hurrying? All right, all right, he's coming!
Anna I think he should always wear white.
Peter (*finishing the boots*) There!

Leonard rises

Your jacket!

Peter struggles to help Leonard out of his jacket, Leonard holding his bat between his legs

Graham This bowler'll be after your blood, I'll tell you that.
Peter Now the bowler at this end tends to pitch them short. So remember what I told you.
Leonard I can't remember anything. Not a thing.
Joan Peter, you'll only confuse him . . .
Graham He's really got his tail up, this bowler . . .
Anna Is there something the matter with Leonard's trousers?

Leonard is scrambling through the wire, helped by Peter from one side, dropping Leonard's jacket by the fence

Graham His next ball'll have your name on, Leonard.
Leonard (*snarling*) Oh, shut your face!
Peter (*squeezing through the wire after Leonard*) Keep calm, now. Keep

calm. (*Following Leonard off*) Remember. Keep your eye on that ball. Don't be afraid to use your feet—and keep that left elbow bent . . .

Leonard and Peter exit

Joan (*climbing back through the wire into the garden and picking up Leonard's jacket*) He's only confusing him. He does the same thing every time I take a driving test . . .
Graham (*looking after them*) Have you ever seen such a sight. He looks like a bell tent with legs.
Anna (*critically*) There's something definitely wrong with those trousers.
Graham Hey, hey. Look at this bowler, polishing the ball. He's after his hat trick. They get that look in their eyes, these bowlers. Last man in, on a hat trick and then in comes Leonard. Like a gift from heaven . . .
Joan Well, give him a chance.
Graham He'll need one.
Anna Oh, look. There he goes. I feel a bit nervous. Isn't that silly?
Joan So do I, for some reason.

Peter enters from the field, breathless

Peter (*climbing through the wire to join them*) I gave him what advice I could. I don't think he was really listening.
Graham You're wasting your breath giving him advice. He never listens to anybody.
Peter Ssshh! There he goes.
Joan Oh, goodness . . .
Graham Look at this little bowler, raring to go. Can't wait to get at him.
Anna Ssshh! Here he comes . . .
Peter If he'll just remember. I only hope he remembers . . .

A slight pause

Graham (*suddenly, very loudly*) Hit up, Leonard!

A cry of "Howzat" is heard, then applause

Joan (*with a cry*) Oh! He's out!
Graham Bowled him.
Peter Oh, no.
Graham First ball. What did I say?
Anna Shouting like that at him. I'm not surprised. You put him off.
Graham Put him off! If that put him off, I'd hate to see him in a test match.
Peter (*sharply, for him*) This doesn't happen to be a test match, does it?
Graham Oh well, *c'est la vie!* (*Moving to the conservatory*) Ah! I think I spy my tea in here.
Anna Are you all stopping now?
Peter No, I think they'll be going in straight away. We'll be fielding for a bit. Give them a few overs before tea. I'd better get back—I hope Leonard hasn't lost heart.

Peter goes

Graham (*at the conservatory door*) I'm having mine in here.
Anna You just wait a minute. Joan, dear?
Joan I'll stay out in the sun, I think, Anna.
Anna (*moving into the house*) Right.

Graham follows Anna

Joan I'll come and help myself.
Anna (*after a pause, to Graham*) Fancy doing that!
Graham What?
Anna Shouting like that, when he was going to hit . . .
Graham He was never going to hit it. He didn't even know where the ball was coming from . . .
Anna Maybe not. You still didn't help . . .

Joan enters the conservatory

Graham That's right. Blame me. Joan. You don't think I put him off deliberately, do you?
Joan (*taking her cup from Anna*) Thank you, Mrs Baker.
Graham Joan, do you think I put Leonard off?
Joan (*coolly*) I don't know. I should ask him. (*To Anna*) I'll take this out then.
Anna Righto, dear.

Joan goes back into the garden and sits in the deck-chair, putting her tea down

Graham I don't know what all the fuss is about, I'm sure. (*Examining the cake*) What's this stuff then?
Anna Cake. Battenburg.
Graham Battenburg? What's the matter with good old Dundee then, all of a sudden?
Anna Nothing's the matter with good old Dundee but after fifteen years of it, I thought you'd like a change for once.
Graham What's got into her, anyway?
Anna Who?
Graham Madam. Sitting out there on her own?
Anna She just likes to get the sun on her.
Graham As long as that's all she wants on her.
Anna Oh, don't be disgusting . . .

Leonard enters from the recreation field. He stands just the other side of the boundary fence. During most of this scene, he has his back to Joan

Graham Hallo, hallo. Jack Hobbs is back.

Leonard (*to Joan*) Hallo.

Joan Hallo. (*After a pause*) Bad luck.

Leonard Yes. (*After a pause*) I've been told to stand here—I'm deep extra cover.

Anna (*calling*) You coming in for tea, Leonard?

Leonard No. I'm fielding.

Anna What?

Leonard I'm fielding.

Anna (*calling*) Oh. (*To Graham*) He's what, did he say.

Graham He's fielding, woman. They've put him there to try and stop them breaking our windows.

Anna Oh.

Graham Seeing we've got him, I think I'll go and order some more glass. Not bad cake this.

Anna Oh. Success.

Graham I still prefer Dundee, though.

Joan By the way. I'm sorry.

Leonard What about?

Joan Well, saying that about you playing for sympathy.

The sound of bat and ball is heard

Graham (*watching the game*) Oh, he hit that one.

Leonard (*wincing from the shot*) I think I probably was, come to think of it.

Joan No. I mean, I asked you to tell me about your wife, didn't I?

Graham That's what I call batting. Four runs all the way . . .

Joan So it's just that it wasn't very nice of me to say that and I'm sorry. That's all.

Leonard That's all right.

Joan You forgive me?

Leonard Of course.

Anna Do you think I should fetch Leonard a pair of your braces for those trousers of his?

Joan What are you thinking?

Leonard I'm just hoping to God this fellow doesn't hit one near me, that's all.

The sound of a mighty shot is heard; Leonard shrinks

Graham (*with a roar of delight*) Hey, that's another one. One bounce and into the road. They'll have that score in ten minutes, at this rate.

Anna I think this cake's a bit stale. I shan't go there, any more.

Joan We were all keeping our fingers crossed for you anyway.

Leonard Yes. So I heard.

Joan Oh. Well. That was him. What do you expect?

Graham Hey. Look at those two. Look at them. What did I say?

Joan You didn't die of embarrassment, anyway. Out there.

Leonard I didn't really have time to.

Joan And you've really done all this because of me?

Leonard No. I was lying. It's always been a childhood ambition of mine to fail dismally for the East Pendon Occasionals.

The sound of bat and ball is heard, and cries of "Look out!"

Joan Are you angry?
Graham That's another big one. Coming this way . . . Leonard!
Leonard You bet I'm . . .
Joan (*in alarm*) Oh, look out . . .
Leonard Oh, crikey Moses . . . (*He runs a little off to meet the ball*)

Groans are heard

Graham Dropped him! That was a chance. A definite chance . . .

Leonard runs back on, holding the ball

Leonard It's because I love you. Is that clear for you . . . ?
Voices (*off*) Hey! Throw it in! Throw the ball!
Graham (*rising and coming into the garden*) What's he holding on to the bloody ball for? Oy! Throw it in. Throw the ball in. They're running five . . .
Joan You'd better throw that back.
Leonard (*discovering the ball in his hand, very irritated by it*) Ohhh!

   Leonard takes a run and exits

Anna comes to the garden door

Graham That'll never make the stumps. Oh, now he's hit someone.
Anna He's hit Peter.
Joan Oh, God . . . (*She gets up and clambers through the fence*)
Graham Killing off his own team, now . . .

   Joan goes off after Leonard

Anna I hope he's all right. He's rolling about, clutching himself . . .
Graham He'll rue the day he ever asked Leonard into this team, I can tell you . . .

   Leonard reappears supporting Peter who limps heavily. Joan scurries along beside them

Leonard I'm terribly sorry.
Joan Are you all right, darling?
Peter Just one side of the knee, it's—aaaahhh!
Anna Oh. Peter. Help him through the fence, Leonard, then he can sit down . . .
Joan Try not to put your weight on it.
Leonard I'm terribly sorry.
Peter That's O.K. Just wasn't expecting a throw in my direction. (*He sits*)
Graham Where did he hit him?
Anna Side of the knee.
Graham That's nasty. I've had that.

Joan Easy now. (*She helps Peter off with his boot*)

Graham With a garden rake.

Peter (*sitting*) It's O.K., darling. I'll be O.K.

Anna Can you still bend it?

Peter I think—aaahhh—no—aaaah!

Anna Oh, dear.

Graham You clumsy ox! Could be a fracture.

Anna Now don't say things like that. You've no way of telling. I think you ought to have it looked at, though.

Peter No, no, I'll be O.K.

Anna Now don't be silly. I think we ought to run you up to the infirmary, don't you, Graham?

Peter No, honestly I—aaaahhh!

Joan Be the best thing, darling.

Anna Probably a bump, but you might as well be certain. It won't take us a second to have it looked at. Graham, help his other side.

Graham I don't think I'll be able to drive in the state I'm in at the moment. Any of that pollen blows into the car . . .

Peter, supported by Graham and Anna, moves towards the house

Anna It's all right. I can drive.

Graham You may have to.

Joan Would you like me to come, darling?

Peter (*as he goes off*) No. No, darling. Stay here, watch the rest of the game. I just want to be dropped there and left. I don't want anyone to come in with me. I'll be fine. It's just a bump.

Anna Gently does it . . .

Graham Mind him through the door.

Peter Just a bump. Nothing. Just a bump.

Leonard I'm terribly sorry.

Anna, Peter and Graham go out into the house

Joan Oh, dear. He does make things difficult . . .

Leonard I don't think this afternoon can be described as one of my most successful, somehow.

Joan No, that was my fault as much as yours. I'm sorry again.

Leonard sits

It looks as if they've decided to go off for tea.

Leonard Or in disgust . . .

Joan You going to join them?

Leonard No. If they want to sing *For He's a Jolly Good Fellow*, they'll have to come over here. I intend to die with my boots off. (*He struggles with his laces and starts to remove his boots*)

Joan Well.

Leonard Well?

Joan I'll say one thing for you.

Leonard What?

Joan You're pretty ruthless in love. Hitting the opposition with a cricket ball.

Leonard That's not the way I do things.

Joan No, I didn't really think it was . . .

Leonard (*wrenching off his second boot*) Oh, that's better. I can feel my feet gulping in breaths of air.

Joan That's an attractive thought.

Leonard (*getting up*) Fancy a paddle.

Joan What?

Leonard (*starting to roll up his trousers, above his knees*) Care for a paddle? Wonderful for fallen arches and thirsty feet . . . (*He steps into the pond*) Ooooh! Ah! That's lovely. Want to join me?

Joan Doesn't look very inviting.

Leonard Nonsense.

Joan I don't know what's in there.

Leonard That's half the fun. Come on, Bernard'll be very hurt if you don't. Come on. It's lovely in.

Joan (*slipping off her sandals*) All right. (*She puts one foot in*) Ugh! What's this at the bottom?

Leonard Don't ask. Just keep paddling. Do you dance?

Joan Mmm?

Leonard (*holding her and shuffling round*) Pond dancing. It's the latest thing . . .

Joan laughs

> "There is a garden in her face
>   Where roses and white lilies blow . . ."

Leonard kisses her gently. He pulls away, then the kiss continues. Leonard breaks away again and sinks to his knees. Joan follows, so that they finish, both kneeling, then lying in the murky water, unaware of anything

> *Especially of Graham, who enters the conservatory from the house. He helps himself to a slice of cake and is about to exit again when he registers on what he has seen. He stops and stares in incredulous horror at Leonard and Joan*

Graham He's at it again. He's at it again. He's at it again . . .

Graham stand shaking and twitching, staring at the lovers, as—

the CURTAIN *falls quickly*

ACT II

SCENE 1

The same. Evening, late autumn

The lights are on in the house. The garden is almost dark, and grows darker during the scene

When the CURTAIN *rises, Anna is discovered in the conservatory watering her plants. Joan sits watching her, slightly restlessly*

Anna I don't think he'll be long. (*She pauses*) I don't know where he's got to.

Joan I expect he'll be here soon.

Anna Oh, I expect so. He should be. (*Examining a plant*) All the leaves keep dropping off this one. I wonder why that is.

Joan How's your bungalow coming on?

Anna What's that, dear?

Joan Your bungalow. How's it coming along?

Anna Oh. You know, it's coming along.

Joan Good.

Anna I don't know why it should do that. (*Back to Joan*) Coming along. (*Concerned*) He should be here by now.

Joan Who?

Anna Leonard.

Joan Oh, yes. Good.

Anna It's this job of his. All hours . . .

Joan Yes.

Anna All weathers. All hours, all weathers . . .

Joan Yes.

Anna Still, he's happy.

Joan Yes.

Anna That's the main thing.

Joan Yes. (*After a pause*) I think he can do better for himself than that, though.

Anna You do?

Joan Than working for the Corporation Parks Department. I mean, he's cut out for something better than that. I told him.

Anna Still, he gets the fresh air, I suppose.

Joan He's not even very good. He spent three days walking round and round the War Memorial raking up leaves. It looks worse than when he started.

Anna Well, it would do. Being autumn.

Joan No, he's cut out for something better. The money's not good either. He's not even qualified.

Anna You don't need to be qualified to rake leaves, surely?

Joan That's the point. If he was a trained gardener he'd be doing something worth while. In the greenhouses or something.

Anna Especially this weather.

Joan I mean, if we're going to finally need somewhere to live eventually —well. We're not just going to do it on the money he's getting now, are we?

Anna Somewhere to live?

Joan Yes.

Anna You mean a house?

Joan Yes.

Anna Buying one, you mean?

Joan Yes.

Anna When did you decide this?

Joan (*slightly embarrassed*) A few days ago.

Anna Oh. Leonard never said anything.

Joan He didn't? Well, we've been looking around a bit. Just looking at prices, you know.

Anna Oh.

Joan I've been going around the estate agents in my lunch breaks.

Anna Have you?

Joan Yes, I've been quite surprised really. I mean, you read a lot about there not being enough houses for people to live in, and prices and things, but honestly. There's masses of places if you take the trouble to look. If you don't turn your nose up at everything, that is. I mean there's a girl I'm working with at the moment and she's just getting married and she has this thing about semi-detached houses. She said she'd sooner live in a cave than a semi. I said to her, what's wrong with a semi, for heaven's sake? They're good enough for most people. When you think about it, a lot of people actually prefer semis, don't they?

Anna I never thought about it.

Joan Or even a terrace. I mean there's some very attractive terraces. It's not everyone wants a detached house, is it? There's so much to keep up, for one thing. And then I should think you could easily get lonely. Suppose Leonard was out working and I was at home. I'd like to feel there were neighbours. I mean, I read about this woman and she was expecting a baby and she had to walk two miles to a call-box to get help, in her condition. That's the nice thing about semis. There's always help there if you need it. Don't you agree?

Anna I'd no idea it had got this far.

Joan How do you mean?

Anna You and Leonard. I'd no idea.

Joan Oh. Yes . . .

Anna You've sorted it all out then?

Joan How do you mean?

Anna Well, you and Peter and so on?

Joan We're going to . . .

Anna I think you should. It's only fair. After all these weeks . . .

Joan Yes, we are sorting it out. We'd have done it before—only Lenny. He didn't want to hurt Peter . . .

Anna All this secret carrying on. It's upsetting everybody. I mean, I have to cross the road if I see Peter's mother. Not that I know her to speak to, really. And I don't need to tell you what it's done to Graham. He's hardly been to work at all. What with following Leonard . . .

Joan Yes, we've seen him . . .

Anna It's getting a thing with Graham. I found him the other night, lying on the cold floor in his pyjamas, listening—I thought he'd had a stroke.

Joan He ought to mind his own business.

Anna Yes, well, I think he feels it is, you see.

Leonard enters from the house. He is dressed in his parks department overalls and no shoes

Leonard Oh, you're here. Hallo! (*Seeing Joan*) Oh, hallo.

Joan Hallo, Lenny.

Leonard Ah!

Anna Have you taken those boots off?

Leonard (*holding up a foot*) Yes.

Anna As long as you have. He trails half the park in here, Joan

Joan He needs some slippers.

Leonard No, I don't.

Joan You do.

Leonard I never wear them.

Joan If you're good, I'll buy you some.

Leonard I don't like bedroom slippers.

Joan You'll wear holes in your socks.

Anna He'd never wear bedroom slippers, even as a little boy. Mother was always saying, Leonard, where's your slippers? He used to lose them on purpose.

Leonard I used to burn them in the boiler.

Anna That's right, burn them in the boiler.

Leonard My bid for individuality.

Anna The whole house stank of burning rubber.

Joan If I spend money on bedroom slippers for you, you'd better not burn them. Just let me see you try . . .

Leonard No. Any slippers you bought me, I'd have stuffed and mounted over the mantelpiece.

Anna Would you both like a cup of tea?

Leonard Please.

Anna We'll eat when Graham comes. He's always late on a Friday.

Joan Working?

Leonard Boozing.

Anna He likes his Friday get-togethers.

Leonard An evening of Graham Baker's jokes at the saloon bar. What a thrilling experience. No wonder the place is half empty.

Anna Nonsense.

Leonard The landlord's thinking of suing Graham for loss of business. He reckons he's employed by a rival brewery.

Anna Take no notice. Did you want a cup, Joan?

Joan I'd love one, Mrs Baker

Anna (*going*) You should go and have a drink occasionally, Leonard. Be a bit more sociable.

Leonard I'm very happy here, Anna. As long as he isn't.

Anna exits, closing the door

Joan I'm glad you don't.

Leonard What?

Joan Drink very much. I don't like men who drink too much.

Leonard I don't think anybody does, really.

Joan Well? Do I get a kiss, then?

Leonard (*amiably*) Oh, yes. With pleasure.

They kiss

Joan Had a hard day?

Leonard Can you tell?

Joan Stupid.

Leonard How was your day, then?

Joan Oh. All right. You know.

Leonard Ah. Nice surprise. You being here.

Joan Yes.

Leonard Nobody saw you?

Joan No. I came in the back way. Crawled through the fence, as usual.

Leonard Ah.

Joan With any luck, for the last time. I came to see you hadn't forgotten.

Leonard What?

Joan I know you. If it suits you . . . Peter. He's coming round at seven.

Leonard Yes, I know.

Joan Tonight.

Leonard Yes.

Joan So you'd better get changed before then, hadn't you?

Leonard Changed?

Joan Before you talk to Peter . . .

Leonard I can talk to him like this.

Joan Well, I'd have thought if you were going to . . .

Leonard I can tell him about us in overalls. All boils down to the same thing. Adds a certain dignity even.

Joan Oh, forget it.

Leonard I'll put on a dinner jacket if you like.

Joan Forget I spoke.

Leonard I told him I wanted to talk about the football match.

Joan As long as you get round to talking about us, eventually.

Leonard Hope he's not too upset . . .

Joan Oh, Leonard.

Leonard Well, I think it might come as a bit of a bolt from the blue.

Joan Not that much.

Leonard How do you mean?

Joan Well.

Leonard He doesn't suspect anything, does he?

Joan It's quite possible he has some idea, Lenny. I mean, I've hardly been near him for months. Mind you, he's as bad as you, in some ways. Ignoring what he prefers not to know . . .

Leonard We've been very careful.

Joan Careful? I'm sick and tired of creeping about.

Leonard I don't know. Been quite fun.

Joan Maybe for you.

Leonard Haven't you enjoyed it?

Joan It's different for a woman.

Leonard Is it?

Joan They prefer to be a little more open about things. Not spend their time ruining their clothes, crawling about behind the war memorial . . .

Leonard laughs

It's not funny, Leonard. I've had enough of it. There is a limit. No matter how much you may love somebody.

Leonard I'll tell him.

Joan What with that brother-in-law of yours. Following us everywhere . . .

Leonard (*kneeling*) "It warms the very sickness in my heart
That I shall live and tell him to his teeth
This didst I . . ."

Joan Oh, Lenny.

Anna comes in with two cups of tea and sugar

Anna You take milk, don't you, Joan?

Joan Please.

Anna Would you like to stay for a meal?

Joan No. I have to go soon, Peter's coming round.

Anna Here?

Leonard Yes.

Anna Why's that?

Joan Leonard's going to tell him.

Anna Oh. I see. (*To Leonard*) You're going to tell Peter.

Leonard Yes.

Anna Why's Leonard telling him?

Joan Because he wants to. Don't you, Lenny?

Leonard Yes.

Anna Well, it's none of my business, but . . .

Graham's voice is heard, off

Graham (*off; calling*) Anna!

Anna Oh, he's back.

Graham (*off*) Anna! Where have you got to?

Anna (*calling*) We're out here, dear! I'd better start cooking. Will Peter want anything?

Leonard I don't imagine he will, no.

Graham enters

Graham What are you doing out here? I—oh. (*He sees Joan and Leonard*) You two, eh?

Leonard Looks like it.

Graham Love's young dream.

Joan Evening, Mr Baker.

Graham Evening, Joan. And what brings Joan round here—or shouldn't I ask?

Joan I just looked in.

Graham Come to pick up a few gardening tips, have you?

Joan Yes, that's right.

Graham Bloody Bachelor of Arts, sweeping up leaves for a living.

Anna Now, Graham, don't start as soon as you come in.

Leonard It's all right. We excuse him.

Graham Eh?

Leonard Seeing as he's drunk.

Graham Now, that's enough of that . . .

Anna Now, why don't you all come in the other room. It's warmer.

No reply

There's a fire in there.

Leonard We're fine here.

Anna Graham?

Graham Uh?

Anna (*softly*) Come on.

Graham No. I'm fine here, too. I prefer it out here.

Anna (*giving up*) Oh, well. I'll get your meal. I'll call you.

Graham What is it?

Anna Haddock.

Graham (*incredulously*) Haddock?

Anna Smoked. If you don't like it, you can leave it.

Graham You certainly dig 'em up, don't you? Haddock.

Anna (*going*) What else do you expect on a Friday?

Anna goes out

Graham What's wrong with cod, all of a sudden? It was good enough for my father.

Leonard That's not saying much. So were you, apparently.

Graham I beg your pardon?

Leonard Evening.

Graham I want a word with you two.

Leonard Oh, yes?

Graham Well, I hope you're thoroughly ashamed of yourselves.

Joan I beg your pardon?

Graham I wouldn't know where to put my face if I were you two. Carrying on like you are . . .

Joan Like what?

Graham I've seen you.

Leonard We've noticed.

Graham Eh?

Leonard We've been aware of your beady little piggy eyes.

Graham Yes, well, I could hardly help but notice . . .

Leonard Even dusted off your binoculars, haven't you. Hasn't had those out since they closed the Teachers' Training College.

Graham What do you mean by that?

Leonard Every bush—every hedge—there he is, peering out. Dirty old man . . .

Graham There's no need to be offensive.

Leonard I could get you arrested, you know. One look at your old mackintosh, they'd have you inside like that . . .

Graham Kissing and cuddling in corners. Public places. It's disgusting. Don't you think you're a bit old for that?

Joan Thank you very much.

Graham I'm talking about him. Now listen, there are people in this neighbourhood . . .

Leonard And what do you . . .

Joan Now don't start again, please.

Graham Right. Right. I will just say one thing, however. That boy has to know. Young Peter. He's a dead loss in my office at the moment, I can tell you. Mooning around, looking like yesterday's breakfast. He's a right to know. I mean, he's my employee. I pay him to work. Not sit about like a sick cabbage. He has to be told.

Leonard He will be.

Graham Yes, but when? That's the point, when?

Leonard This evening.

Graham Oh. Well. Not before time. Been going on for months.

Leonard Satisfied?

Graham Just a minute. Are you going to be here when he finds out?

Leonard I'm telling him.

Graham You're telling . . . (*Laughing*) He'll tear you in pieces.

Leonard Nonsense.

Graham Limb from limb . . .

Joan Don't talk rubbish.

Graham Well, I'm not standing anywhere near. He's been itching to get his hands on someone. You can see him. He's been building up . . .

Joan I don't know why you're saying this.

Graham What? Carrying on with his girl behind his back. His so-called friend? He'll go raving mad . . .

Leonard Nonsense.

Graham God help you. That's all I can say. God help you.

Joan It'll be nothing like that at all. Leonard is simply going to explain the facts to Peter and then Leonard and I are . . .

Graham And then Leonard and you what? What happens then?

Joan Leonard and I will probably get married.

Graham You and what's left of him, you mean. Do you take this bag of pieces to be your lawful wedded husband . . . ? (*He laughs, gleeful*)

Joan Leonard and I will buy somewhere and settle down like any other normal happy couple . . .

Graham Normal couple? With him? You're hopeful.

Joan I don't know why you keep picking on him. There's nothing out of the ordinary about Leonard. He's perfectly normal. I wish you'd stop making out he's something peculiar. All Lenny wants, all I want, is to be happily married and share our lives together. Maybe even have children—who knows?

Graham But he's been through all that once already, my dear.

Joan That was just one of those things. Anyone can make mistakes. Lenny, speak up for yourself, for goodness' sake.

Leonard Oh, yes. Yes.

Joan Yes what?

Leonard Fine.

Joan What do you mean, fine?

Leonard Fine, yes.

Joan That's all Leonard wants. That's all I want.

Graham You mean to tell me, you are going to train him to go out to work every day, earn money, come home to you again every night?

Joan It's not a matter of training . . .

Graham You stand more chance with a camel . . .

Joan Look, I don't think you've any right to . . . Leonard, will you stand up for yourself, for heaven's sake . . .

Leonard I think I'll just go for a walk.

Joan What?

Leonard Just a stroll.

Joan Now?

Leonard Quick one. (*He steps over Graham's feet to the conservatory door*)

Joan But Peter'll be here . . .

Leonard I'll just be outside.

Joan Well, don't go far, darling, will you?

Leonard No—no.

Leonard goes out into the garden. He wanders down to the fence, after a moment, climbs through and disappears into the field

Graham Now, look here, Joan, you're making the biggest mistake of your life.

Joan I don't think so.

Graham I do.

Joan I think I'd better be going. (*She starts to rise*)

Graham Just a minute, Joan. Joan, just a minute. Look, you're a nice girl. You're a decent girl. Do you realize what you're taking on with him?

Joan Of course I do.

Graham He doesn't need a wife, he needs a nurse.

Joan Now look . . .

Graham Oh, I've joked about him. I've had a laugh about him in the past, as much as anybody. But I'm serious now. He's not responsible, let's face it. There's been moments in this house when we've come damn close to having him put away altogether. Do you want to tie yourself for life to a man who jabbers away to gnomes?

Joan That's because he's lonely.

Graham Don't give me that. If he was lonely he'd have had the decency to give the neighbours the time of day. Instead of carrying on like he does. Do you know they're frightened to sit out at all next door. Because of him. They're retired folk on a fixed income. They've got enough worries making ends meet without having Leonard peering at them through knot-holes in the fence every time they bring a deck-chair out.

Joan I don't know about that.

Graham Yes, well I do. No, you're too good for him, Joan. I won't stand by and see this happen. I won't have it.

Joan What do you plan to do then?

Graham Well, I don't think I need do anything, as it happens. I think Peter's capable of taking care of himself.

Joan So's Leonard.

Graham God help us! Bloody female intuition. If there's a wrong man they'll pick him. Every time.

Joan Well, we're hardly spoilt for choice, are we?

Graham Eh?

Anna and Peter come in

Anna They're all out here, Peter, for some reason, I . . . (*She stops as she sees Graham and Joan*) Oh.

Peter Hallo!

Graham Oh, hallo, Peter.

Peter I didn't know you were going to be here, Joan?

Joan Yes.

Peter I see.

Anna Where's Leonard?

Graham Outside.

Anna What's he up to now?

Graham You'd better call him, hadn't you? Tell him Peter's here.

NO 1 ON

Anna Yes. (*She goes into the garden, closing the door, and walks slowly down to the fence*)

Peter He wanted a word with me.

Graham So I believe. So I believe. Well, I think we'd better leave you to it. Eh, Joan?

Joan Yes.

Graham I'll give you a lift home.

Joan No, that's all right.

Graham No. It won't take a second. Can't have you walking . . .

Anna (*calling*) Leonard!

Graham I'll get the car out. (*Going out*) Get my coat . . .

Joan All right.

Graham goes out

(*Gathering her coat; to Peter*) Good night, then.

Peter Good night. Joan . . .

Joan Yes?

Peter Nothing.

Joan Right.

Peter I hear you make quite a habit of coming here, these days . . .

Joan Oh, yes? Well, maybe I do. So?

Peter I see. Well, I might see you . . .

Joan You might. Good night.

Joan goes into the house

Peter stands brooding

Leonard returns from the field

Anna Where have you been?

Leonard Just checking our goal-posts. We put them up today.

Anna You haven't got any shoes on. Your supper's nearly ready.

Leonard Lovely.

Anna And Peter's here.

Leonard Oh. Is he? Good.

Anna Leonard . . .

Leonard Mmmm?

Anna Be nice and tactful, won't you?

Leonard Naturally.

Anna arrives at the door of the house. Leonard follows

Hallo there.

Peter Hallo.

Anna My word, you're looking well, Peter.

Peter Am I?

Anna Yes. Don't you think so, Leonard? Isn't Peter looking well?

Leonard Great. He looks great.

Peter Thanks.

Anna Well. I've got a supper to cook. Better go and cook it, hadn't I? I'll be in the kitchen . . .

Anna goes off

There is a pause. Peter moves behind an upright chair and gently lifts it. Leonard looks out of the window

Leonard Good view of the Plough, tonight.

Peter The what?

Leonard The Plough. Ursa Major. Up there. Stars . . .

Peter (*putting down the chair and looking up*) Oh, yes?

Leonard At least, I think it's the Plough. It might possibly be Cassiopeia. I know one looks like a W upside down and one doesn't. I know that. The one that doesn't looks like a saucepan upside down. (*He leans on a folding chair, which collapses*)

Peter I didn't know Joan would be here.

Leonard (*leaning the chair against the wall*) No?

Peter You didn't say.

Leonard (*opening a drawer in the chest*) No. Well, she—dropped in. That's all.

Peter Ah.

Leonard As a matter of fact . . . (*He pulls out a hammer*)

Peter What?

Leonard It was Joan I wanted to talk to you about . . .

Peter I'd rather you didn't.

Leonard But it's a bit important.

Peter I'd rather not discuss Joan at the moment, if you don't mind. I appreciate it. But I'd rather you didn't.

Leonard Oh. (*He replaces the hammer and opens another drawer, noisily*)

Peter What are you looking for?

Leonard (*starting*) Nothing. Nothing.

Peter What about this football, then?

Leonard Football?

Peter You said you wanted to talk about it.

Leonard Yes.

Peter Have you changed your mind?

Leonard Yes.

Peter Good. That's great news. I was afraid you'd let us down.

Leonard Goodness, no. Look, Peter, I think all the same we ought to talk about Joan—if you don't mind . . .

Peter I'm sorry, Len. I've said I don't want to discuss her.

Leonard I know but . . .

Peter This is a personal matter.

Leonard Exactly. I know. That's just the . . .

Peter Just don't push me, that's all. I'm a reasonable person. You know that. But when I was a child, I realized what a terrible temper I had. I've managed to control it ever since. Despite everything, I've managed to keep it under control. But it's been a battle at times, I can tell you. And when it comes to Joan . . .

Leonard Yes, I realize. I just thought a few words . . .

Peter For the last time, keep out of this, Leonard.

Leonard It was only . . .

Peter I'm warning you, don't put too much a strain on our friendship. You can push it too far, you know, if you're not careful . . .

Leonard Ah.

Anna enters with a cup of tea

Anna Brought you a cup of tea, Peter. (*She puts it down on the table in silence, aware of an atmosphere, and collects up the empty cups and sugar*) Both warm enough in here, are you? Yes, it's quite mild to-night. Considering . . . All right? Good . . .

Anna goes back to the kitchen

Leonard Well. That's it.

Peter Yes. Seems to be.

Leonard Glad it's cleared up, anyway. You've taken it—very well.

Peter (*still bitter*) Hardly much choice, had I?

Leonard No. (*He produces a cardboard box and board from the drawers*) Ah!

Peter What's that?

Leonard My old draughts-board.

Peter Draughts?

Leonard I haven't seen this for ages. Used to play with Mother. She was a demon. Huff you as soon as look at you.

Peter Good game.

Leonard Yes. (*Tentatively*) Do you fancy a quick tournament?

Peter Well . . . bit rusty. Probably forgotten how to play.

Leonard Same here.

Peter Right you are.

Leonard Great . . .

They start to lay out the board on the table

Peter I used to play with my old granddad. When he was alive, that was.

Leonard Oh, yes!

Peter He's dead, now.

Leonard Oh. Well. He's probably got better things to do. (*He puts a white and a black piece behind his back*)

Graham appears above the wall with a pair of binoculars

Graham (*furtively*) Anna! Come on. Here!

Leonard Which hand?
Peter Left.
Leonard White. Right. Your start.
Peter Right.

They settle down for the game

Graham Anna!

Anna joins Graham

Anna What are you playing at?
Graham I want to watch this. I wouldn't miss this . . .
Anna Why don't you let them alone . . .
Graham You say there was an atmosphere in there?
Anna Oh, yes. You could have cut it with a knife.
Graham I bet there was. I bet there was.
Leonard (*observing Peter's opening move*) Ah-ha. Standard Viennese Open-
  ing gambit, eh. Right, it calls for the Mandarin defence, I feel. (*Moving
  a piece*) Ha!
Graham Can you see what they're up to?
Anna A bit. I don't like this. What if they see us?
Graham Don't worry. They'll be far too busy.

Peter moves a piece

Anna They're both sitting down.
Graham I know they're sitting down. What are they doing?
Anna I can't see.
Graham Come round here, woman, come round here.

*Graham and Anna move round the wall to the fence. Leonard moves a
piece*

Peter Oh, crafty move!

Anna comes over the fence to below the pond

Anna I think they're playing draughts.
Graham (*incredulously*) Playing draughts? How the hell can they be
  playing draughts. He should be wiping the floor with him. (*Fiddling
  with his binoculars*) Damn and blast these things!
Leonard Peter, there's something very odd about this game.
Peter What do you mean?
Leonard It's impossible for anyone to win.
Peter What do you mean? It's possible to win at draughts.
Leonard Not when you're playing on the white squares and I'm playing
  on the black. I can't take you and you can't take me!

They both start laughing

Anna They're both laughing.
Graham Laughing? I'll give them draughts and laughing. (*He comes over*

the fence, pushes past Anna, and goes to the conservatory) Get out of the way, woman! (*He storms into the conservatory*)

Peter and Leonard continue to laugh as they turn to see him. Leonard falls sideways off his seat, still laughing. Graham rushes out into the garden

Anna What's going on in there?
Graham How the hell should I know what's going on! How the hell . . .

CURTAIN

SCENE 2

The same. The following day, Saturday, noon, cold and clear

Graham is alone in the conservatory. He is speaking into the telephone, reading deliberately from a scrap of paper in his hand. The receiver has a handkerchief jammed into the mouthpiece

Graham Hallo—hallo—this is a well-wisher. I think you should know that your fiancée is at present carrying on an amorous relationship with a certain Mr Leonard . . . How was that? . . . Hallo. Are you listening? . . . Anna? . . . Anna, are you there? Can you hear me? . . . Where have you gone . . . ?

Anna enters

Anna I don't think that phone's working out there. I can't hear you at all.
Graham Oh, my God . . .
Anna You've got that thing stuffed up it. No wonder I can't hear you.
Graham I know I have. This is to muffle my voice.
Anna It certainly did that.
Graham Well, that's a wash-out. (*He removes the handkerchief and replaces the receiver*)
Anna Be quicker to send Peter a postcard.
Graham (*thoughtfully*) Something to muffle the voice . . .
Anna Peter'll be round here to play football in a minute. Why don't you tell him then.
Graham I'm not getting myself any further involved in this. Thank you very much. There's quite enough mud rubbed off as it is.
Anna Then leave them to sort it out for themselves.
Graham What, you mean the way Leonard did last night? Not on your life. I'm putting no more trust in him. That man has systematically destroyed everyone he's touched. He's turned Peter into a sullen lout, a nice girl like Joan into someone who's no better than she should be and me into a laughing stock. On top of that he has scandalized every decent

person in the neighbourhood. They've all seen it. Every one of them. All except Peter that is. Someone has to tell him. He has a right to know.

Anna I'll tell him then.

Graham What?

Anna If you like.

Graham You'll do nothing of the kind. You'll keep well out of it. We'll do this my way. (*Picking up a teacup and speaking into it*) Hallo . . . hallo . . . what does that sound like? Listen, I'll tell you something else. Do you know how old that girl Joan is? I found out the other day. She's twenty-three—twenty-three. (*He picks up the receiver and speaks into the cup and the mouthpiece simultaneously*) Hallo . . .

Anna Yes, I thought she was about that . . .

Graham Hallo, hallo . . . (*He puts down the receiver and teacup*) Nearly it. And how old's Leonard?

Anna Well, he'll be . . .

Graham I'll tell you exactly how old he is. He's not much younger than me. A man can't carry on love affairs with young girls at my age—his age, can he? He's not going to. It's not right. I won't have it. He's not fit to have a girl like that. He's not going to have her. (*Picking up an empty flower-pot, he shouts into it*) Hallo! This is a well-wisher . . . That's it, something deeper. We need something deeper. Get back on that extension phone.

Anna How long do you intend keeping this up?

Graham Come on, woman, come on . . .

Graham goes out to the house

Anna (*following him and getting caught up*) I wish you'd stop stretching this cotton across the doorways. It keeps sticking to my feet.

Anna goes out.

There is a slight pause, then Leonard enters from the field. He wears a scarf, gloves, but no coat, and carries a brown paper parcel. He climbs over the fence and starts to walk towards the house. The silence is broken by Joan's voice off, as she follows him on

Joan (*running on*) Lenny! Lenny! (*Breathlessly*) Thank heavens I caught you. Hallo, darling.

Leonard Hallo.

Joan (*throwing her arms round him and kissing him*) I was right at the top of the hill.

Leonard Were you? (*Waving his parcel*) I've just been collecting these.

Joan What are they?

Leonard Football kit. For this afternoon.

Joan You're still going through with that?

Leonard Well, yes, I promised.

Joan I thought that Peter would—how did it go?

Leonard When?

Joan Last night? How did Peter take it?

Leonard Oh. Awfully well. Awfully well.

Joan Was it terrible for you, darling?

Leonard No. No, not really.

Joan He didn't get . . .

Leonard Violent? No, he—kept himself in check.

Joan (*hugging him*) Oh, Lenny.

Leonard (*looking down stage*) That woman next door's watching us. Behind her curtains.

Joan Let her. She's jealous that's all. She fancies you.

Leonard Have you seen her? She's a hundred and ten if she's a day. I rather hope by that age I'll be comparatively lust-free.

Joan You mean you don't enjoy sex?

Leonard Oh, I enjoy *sex*, it's the lusting bit I don't enjoy very much. It's twice as exhausting and not half as enjoyable.

Joan Don't worry, my darling. Your lusting days are nearly over . . .

Leonard I'm not that old.

Joan Now we're together. (*Kissing him*) I'll be watching you play.

Leonard "Strange fits of passion have I known: And I will dare to tell . . ." er—no . . .

Joan What's that?

Leonard Forgotten the rest. Wordsworth.

Joan Oh. (*She kisses him again*)

Leonard She's still watching.

Joan Who cares, darling? Just think of us.

Leonard Us. Yes.

Joan 'Bye. (*She kisses him again*)

Joan goes, blowing him another kiss

Leonard lingers for a moment, then goes to the conservatory. As he is closing the door he sees the phone off the hook. He picks up the receiver and listens

Leonard Is anybody there? Hallo? . . . Beg your pardon? . . . What's that? . . . Better . . . What's better? . . . I know it sounds like Leonard. I am Leonard. Who's this . . . Anna? . . . What are you doing?

Graham returns holding a large saucepan into which he is speaking. He fails at first to see Leonard

Graham Hallo. Testing. Hallo. This is a well-wisher . . . Hallo. (*Seeing Leonard*) Ah! What are you doing here? (*He drops the saucepan to his side*)

Leonard Having a chat with your wife on the phone, actually.

Graham Ah.

Leonard Where is she?

Graham In the drawing-room.

Leonard (*looking at Graham, then through the open door, then at the phone receiver*) Your marriage breaking up at last, is it?

Graham We were checking the phone for a fault, that's all. Where have you been?

Leonard (*replacing the receiver*) My morning constitutional.

Graham Oh, yes? Since when have you started taking constitutionals.

Leonard About the same time you started talking to yourself inside saucepans.

Graham There's a logical explanation for that.

Leonard Don't tell me. You were checking it for a fault.

Anna enters

Anna Oh, it *was* you I was talking to, Leonard. I thought it was.

Leonard Yes, I enjoyed the chat. (*He picks up the parcel*) Excuse me, won't you?

Graham Where are you going now?

Leonard To change—for the match. And if I get any more bright remarks out of you while I'm out there I'll come over and ram the ball up your nose.

Anna Leonard.

Leonard makes to leave

Graham Hey! Just a minute . . . (*He beckons Leonard, who stays where he is*) Come here. (*He beckons*) Here a minute. (*He beckons*)

Leonard (*still in the doorway*) What?

Graham When you go upstairs you'll see that all your personal belongings have been moved on to the landing.

Leonard They've been what?

Graham I repeat, I have cleared your room of your belongings. You'll find them outside the door on the landing.

Leonard What?

Anna What did you do that for?

Graham We'll be moving to the bungalow shortly. Until then that room is needed for storage. It is no longer available.

Anna Don't be so stupid . . .

Graham I warned him, Anna. Time and time again I warned him. If he carried on behaving like he was, he was out. And he's out, as from today.

Anna I won't have this. He's my brother.

Graham As far as I'm concerned, he's a lodger who's outstayed his welcome.

Anna Now, Graham, if you think . . .

Leonard It's all right, Anna. Don't worry.

Anna If he thinks he . . .

Leonard Anna! Ssh. He's hardly worth talking to and he's certainly not worth arguing with.

Graham Out by tonight.

Leonard A pleasure.

Graham (*somewhat surprised by his victory*) Right . . . right then. As long as that is clear, if you'll excuse me, please.

Graham marches out

Anna (*after a slight pause; furiously*) I think that's absolutely disgraceful. Who the hell does he think he is?

Leonard (*calming her*) Anna . . .

Anna No, well . . .

Leonard Anna—listen, love . . .

Anna What?

Leonard You've always coped with him very well. Don't let him get under your skin now.

Anna No, well . . .

Leonard If you start, you'll only finish up the same as him, you know. His sort of behaviour's catching.

Anna He's never had much effect on me up to now. I don't see why he should start.

Leonard He's changed you more than you think.

Anna How do you mean?

Leonard I don't know. I just remember what you were like before you married him.

Anna You can't blame that on him, dear. Be the same with anyone. That's just fifteen years of trying to cope. I mean we had a wonderful mother, both of us, but she never gave us a clue what to expect later, did she? Either of us.

Leonard I'll see what he's done to my stuff . . .

Anna Are you really going? Where will you go?

Leonard I have plans, don't worry. I have plans.

Anna Leonard.

Leonard Mmm?

Anna These plans of yours. Are you sure you've included everyone that should be included in them?

Leonard Yes. Well—more or less . . .

Anna Now, listen, Leonard, I've never interfered in your personal life in any way, you know that—but I think I really must . . . (*She breaks off*) Oh. Now here's Peter.

Leonard Oh, God. (*He heads for the door*)

Anna Leonard . . .

Leonard Oh, my God.

Leonard goes out

Anna Leonard! (*Sighing, to herself*) He's got all the worst of his mother's side . . .

Peter, jumping over the fence, dressed in his football kit, sees Anna

Peter (*calling*) Hallo, Mrs Baker.

Anna Hallo, Peter.

Peter Was that Leonard just then?

Anna Yes, he's just gone upstairs, I think.

Peter He hasn't forgotten the game, has he?

Anna I don't think he has, no. I think he's changing.

Peter Oh, good. (*Loosening his calf muscles*) I wouldn't put it past Leonard. He's a bit vague sometimes. He let us down rather badly on the darts match.

Anna Did he?

Peter Yes. He went to the wrong pub.

Anna Oh, dear.

Peter (*jumping up and down*) Haven't seen Joan around at all, have you?

Anna No.

Peter Oh. I was rather hoping she might come along. She usually does. Give us some support. They've a damn good centre-forward, I don't know how we'll manage against him.

Anna Peter . . .

Peter (*jumping*) He used to be a pro. Then he got married.

Anna Peter, dear . . .

Peter Gave it all up. For the quiet life.

Anna Peter. (*She takes his arm and stops him jumping*)

Peter Yes?

Anna I just wanted a word with you, actually, Peter. About you and Joan.

Peter (*guarded*) Oh, yes?

Anna Yes. About you. And Joan. And . . .

Peter And what?

Anna I can't really believe you don't know, Peter.

Peter I see. (*Starting to jump again*) Maybe I do.

Anna But you've said nothing about it? To anyone?

Peter No.

Anna I think you should. (*Stopping him again*) I know it's more difficult with someone you know so well—and like.

Peter Yes. It is.

Anna But you must talk it out with him. You really must.

Peter It's just I've got so much anger in me—(*punching his hand*)—Mrs Baker. That's the trouble. You see, I'm a basically violently jealous type. There have been times when I've fought men, physically, for Joan—you see?

Anna Well, that's probably better than nursing a grudge, isn't it?

Peter You think I should tackle him, then?

Anna The sooner the better, I should think.

Peter (*with sudden decision*) You're right, Mrs Baker. Of course you're right. I should have said something months ago. I mean, it's not fair on anyone, is it? Least of all you. Heaven knows what you must have been going through.

Anna Me?

Peter It can't have been easy for you.

Anna Well . . .

Peter You must still be very fond of him.

Anna Well, I am. And I've stood by him as best I could in the past, Peter. But he has to stand up for himself and face things eventually. For his own sake.

Peter (*holding out his hand*) I think you're a very wonderful person, Mrs Baker.

Anna Oh. (*She shakes his hand*) Well, thank you.

Peter (*pumping*) If you don't mind my saying so, I hope to God in the future, if I ever need anyone to stand by me, she'll be someone like you.

Anna (*flattered but bewildered*) That's a very nice thing to say, thank you . . . (*She takes her hand away*)

Leonard enters from the house. He is now wearing football shirt, shorts and boots, and an old sports jacket. He carries a battered book

Peter Hallo.

Leonard I don't know how you both feel about the subject, but I'm particularly averse to people who ill-treat books. In hurling my belongings into the passage, your husband has successfully bent, twisted, dirtied or just simply destroyed every damn book I own. If there's one thing I cannot stand, it's cruelty to books. I'm not too keen on cruelty to animals or children either, but especially to bloody books . . .

Anna Leonard! You're getting like Graham.

Leonard (*calming*) So I am. I do beg your pardon. That would never do. Two of us and the Almighty is quite likely to look down, admit failure and cancel the world.

Anna Yes, well, I think I'll just pop in for a second . . .

Peter Leonard . . .

Anna See what Graham's up to.

Leonard (*thumbing through his book*) Haven't read this for ages.

Peter (*taking off his track suit and draping it over the fence*) I wonder if I could have a word with you, Leonard?

Leonard Certainly. Pick a nice one.

Anna That's right. It's a nice day for your game. Think it should stay like it.

Peter Yes.

Anna Don't mind me. I'll just get on. It's nice and quiet out here. (*Going into the conservatory*) I'll shut the door. Then you'll be on your own.

Anna closes the door behind her and with one last apprehensive look, goes into the house

Peter I've just been having a word with Anna.

Leonard Oh, yes?

Peter She's quite a person . . .

Leonard She certainly is.

Peter About me and Joan. She thinks it's time things came to a show-down.

Leonard (*lowering his book*) She does?

Peter I told her, if it actually came to it, I've got such a violent temper—someone's liable to get killed. I mean that, literally.

Leonard Ah.

Peter But anything's better than nursing a grudge, isn't it? Don't you agree?

Leonard I—don't know. I mean—I think there's no harm in nursing the odd grudge, occasionally.

Peter Look, Leonard, I'm not all that stupid, you know. This has been going on for two months. It wasn't hard to put two and two together. She's spent more time in this house in the last few weeks than she has in her own. You don't have to be a mind-reader. But what I hate most about this whole business, Len, is the mean, dirty way it's been conduc-ted. And that I'll never forgive. I won't forgive any man who's brought someone as pure as Joan down to his own cheap nasty level.

Leonard Oh, I don't know about that . . .

Peter Every sordid thing you could think of. Binoculars, dirty mackin-toshes, touching her up in public . . . I'll never forgive him for that.

Leonard Who?

Peter I warn you, if I get near him—if I get near him . . .

Leonard Who?

Peter It's no good, Leonard; you can't protect him any longer. Not even your own brother-in-law. You can't go on being loyal for the rest of your life. Not to someone like that.

Leonard (*alarmed*) I see your point, yes, I see your point . . .

Peter All right, you tell me. What should I do? What would you do?

Leonard Me? Well, I—I'd—er . . .

Peter Should I just carry on: Yes, Mr Baker, no, Mr Baker—as if nothing was wrong? Or should I get him up against a wall and give him what someone like that deserves? You tell me. You tell me.

Leonard Why not? Yes, why not? (*He sits on the bench*)

A slight pause

Peter (*calming down slightly*) Is that what you'd do?

Leonard Well, people tend to vary but . . .

Peter (*sitting next to Leonard*) Of course you would. (*Clapping Leonard on the shoulder*) You know something, Len, we're the same, you and me. Underneath, we're the same. And there comes a time when people like us, the ones that get pushed around, we've got to get together and say—(*thumping Leonard's knee*)—no. No—(*he thumps Leonard's knee*)—to——

Leonard covers his knee with his book

—little tyrants and petty dictators who take advantage of their class and their money and their so-called position. (*He stands up and moves away*) We've got to stand up and say—to hell with them.

Leonard Hear, hear.
Peter Let's say it, then.
Leonard Er—to hell with them.
Peter And together . . .
Both To hell with them.

Graham enters from the house

Graham (*opening the garden door, laughing*) Hallo, hallo. It's Bobby
Moore. What's he want?
Peter No, it's me.
Graham So it is. (*Towards Leonard*) Look at him. What does he look like.

*Leonard does not reply. Instead he motions Peter forward and sits on the
bench*

Peter Come on then.

Leonard reads his book

Graham Eh?
Peter I said come on.
Graham What? Oh, tackle you, you mean? Well, I haven't got the right
boots on for it but . . . (*He prances about doing fancy footwork*) Hup—
hup—hey-hup—come on then, hup—hup.
Peter (*pushing Graham back*) I'm not talking about football.
Graham Oh? Aren't you? Well, that's what you're dressed for or didn't
you realize? (*He prances forward*)
Peter I'm talking about beating the daylights out of you. (*He pushes
Graham back*)
Graham Eh?
Peter Come on.
Graham (*to Leonard*) What's he on about, Leonard?
Leonard No idea.
Peter Come on. You want her, you'll have to do better than that.
Graham Want her? Want who? Leonard, what's he talking about?
Leonard Just a sec. Just let me finish this chapter.
Graham Leonard!

Peter grabs him by the throat

(*Choking*) Haaah! Leonard! Leonard!
Peter (*shaking him like a rag-doll*) Come on then. Let's see you fight. Let's
see you fight. Come on.
Graham Help!

Anna enters and runs to them

Anna Graham! Peter, what are you doing? Peter, stop it. (*She hits at him
without effect*) Peter! Leonard, stop him.
Peter (*under this*) Fight, fight—come on, fight.

Graham gurgles

Anna Leonard, what's he doing?
Leonard I think he's trying to kill him actually.

Joan comes in from the recreation field. She carries a paper bag

Joan (*she takes in the scene*) Leonard? Peter, stop it. Peter! PETER!

Peter stops, under Joan's influence. Graham falls to the ground

   (*Soothingly, as if Peter were a cornered tiger*) That's it, Peter. That's it, quietly now. Quietly. That's enough.

Anna tends Graham

Graham (*who appears to have lost his voice*) Oh, good grief.
Anna You all right, dear?
Graham I think he's damaged my vocal chords.
Anna How did this all start? Leonard?
Leonard (*innocently*) No idea.
Anna Well, somebody must have said something.
Peter It's not what they say, it's what they did.
Anna Well, Graham hasn't done anything, dear.
Peter Hasn't done anything? What do you mean, hasn't done anything?
Anna Well, it's between you and Leonard, surely.
Peter Leonard?
Anna Well, he's the one who's—you didn't think it was Graham? You can't have done? Graham and Joan? Joan and Graham?
Peter Of course it was him and her, who else was she . . . (*He pauses*)

Leonard turns over a page

Joan Who told you that?
Peter No-one did. I knew. I found out. It wasn't Leonard. I mean, it's not you and Leonard we're talking about—Leonard? It wasn't you and Joan, was it?

A pause

Joan (*to Leonard*) You mean, you let him—you let Peter nearly . . . ?
Leonard I was reading my book. I didn't really notice.
Peter Leonard?
Leonard Well—I'm sorry. Yes, in that case. It was me.
Peter (*shaking his head and jumping up and down*) I'd better loosen up. Kick-off in five minutes.

Peter goes, jumping over the fence

Leonard Managed to tell him at last. (*He smiles feebly at Joan*)
Graham He's a homicidal maniac.
Anna Don't talk, dear. Don't talk . . .

Graham He's fired. He should be locked up. I'm firing him. (*To Leonard*)
This is your doing, this is. All your doing, you . . .

Anna Come on. (*She guides him to the conservatory*) We'll get you upstairs
and you can have a nice gargle and a lie down.

Graham (*as he goes, pointing an accusing finger back at Leonard*) You.
You're responsible. It was you—you . . . (*his voice has gone*)

Anna and Graham go into the house

Joan Have you got what you wanted?

Leonard How do you mean?

Joan I mean the pleasure of seeing your brother-in-law nearly choked to
death.

Leonard I didn't want that, really. It just sort of happened.

Joan Graham was right. There are a lot of things that just sort of happen
when you're around, aren't there? (*Taking Leonard's book*) Well. That's
it, isn't it?

Leonard How do you mean?

Joan I mean I'm going. That's what I mean.

Leonard (*lamely*) Do you have to?

Joan Well, one thing's certain, isn't it? Whatever it is you did want, it
wasn't me.

Leonard I wouldn't say that.

Joan Oh, Lenny! Even today, with all this, you still couldn't tell Peter.

Leonard It was difficult. I mean it was either a case of Peter being hurt,
when he found it was me—and then me being hurt when he did—or
Graham. When I weighed it up . . . (*He pauses*)

Joan What about me; Leonard? What about me?

Leonard You? I didn't think it would really affect you. I mean . . .

Joan Oh, forget it. Forget it.

Leonard I mean him thinking it was Graham seemed sort of right somehow. Poetic justice, I suppose . . .

Joan (*measuredly, looking at him*) Yes. Well, we don't all happen to be
bloody poets, do we. (*She flings his book in the pond*)

Joan turns and goes quickly into the house

*Leonard retrieves his book, tries to straighten it, and lays it down. He sees
the parcel Joan has left, sits on the bench, looks into the paper bag and
cautiously opens it. He brings out a pair of gaily coloured bedroom slippers.
He frowns at them, then, after a second, places them gingerly on the edge
of the pond and launches them with a gentle shove*

Leonard (*sadly, regarding his improvised boats*) "All's over then: Does truth
sound bitter as one first believes? Hark, 'tis the . . ." (*He pauses, frowns
and shakes his head*)

Peter enters from the recreation field, jumping over the fence

Peter Has she gone?
Leonard Yes.
Peter Ah. Thought she might.

They stand awkwardly

No hard feelings, by the way.
Leonard Mmmm?
Peter No hard feelings. A fair fight.
Leonard Ah.
Peter Yes. (*Depressed again*) Only we both seem to have lost.
Leonard I wouldn't say that . . .
Peter No?
Leonard I'd say we just seem to have mislaid the trophy, that's all.
Peter Yes. (*He ponders*) Still, there's more to life than winning trophies.
    That's what I say.
Leonard Very well put.

The referee's whistle blows

Peter Thank you. (*Punching Leonard on the shoulder*) Hey . . .
Leonard (*startled, thinking his time has come*) What?
Peter Are you playing in this stupid football match or aren't you?
Leonard Oh, yes, right. Sorry.
Peter Only there's twenty-two of us standing out there waiting to start.
    Kick-off was five minutes ago.
Leonard Okay then. Off we go.

*They fool. Leonard kicks an imaginary stone and follows it. Peter moves in
to tackle. Leonard kicks Peter's ankle. Peter stands bolt upright, smiling*

Leonard What's wrong?
Peter It's my ankle—nothing.
Leonard I'm so sorry . . .
Peter Nothing, nothing at all. (*Leaning on Leonard*) Just help me on. I'll
    be all right.
Leonard Are you sure?
Peter (*as they go off*) I'm fine. I'm fine, don't bother, I'm fine. Just get me
    on. Just get me on the field.

*Leonard, gesticulating to the other players, with Peter leaning on his
shoulders limping heavily, makes his way on to the football field, as*

the CURTAIN *falls*

FURNITURE AND PROPERTY LIST

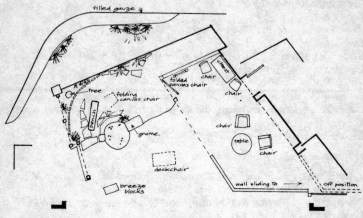

ACT I

SCENE 1

On stage: GARDEN:
Bench
Pile of breeze blocks
Lawn-mower
Gnome with fishing-rod
Tree
Pond filled with murky water

CONSERVATORY:
2 upright chairs
Wicker armchair
Wooden armchair
Circular table. *On it:* false top with cloth and doyley
Canvas chair (folded against wall)
Chest of drawers. *In drawers:* hammer, set of draughtsmen and board,
    dressing. *On it:* telephone
On walls, floor, shelves: garden dressing, including many pot plants
    in various stages of decay, trowels, trugs, watering cans, etc.

Off stage: Cigar end and glass of Scotch (**Graham**)
Tray with 1 plate of biscuits, 1 slop basin, 1 sugar basin, 5 saucers,
    5 teacups, 5 teaspoons, 5 table napkins (**Joan**)
Teapot and milk jug (**Anna**)
5 tea plates (**Joan**)
Plate of sandwiches (**Graham**)
Spare pot of tea (**Anna**)

Personal: **Peter:** watch

SCENE 2

Strike: Cigar from pond
           Whisky glass
           All cups and saucers
           False table top
           Lawn-mower

Set: Folding canvas chair open above pond
           Deck-chair below pond
           Joan's robe by deck-chair
           Sun oil by robe
           Inflated cushion at top end of robe
           Graham's sandals in deck-chair
           Knitting for Anna

Off stage: Cricket bat (**Leonard**)
             Tray with 1 plate of Battenburg cake, 4 teacups, 4 saucers, 4 tea-
                 spoons, milk jug, sugar basin, teapot
             Cricket ball (**Leonard**)

Personal: **Graham:** handkerchief

ACT II

SCENE 1

Strike: Leonard's boots, socks and cap
           Peter's boot
           Knitting
           Deck-chair, cushion
           Tea things

Set: Watering can, trowel and newspaper on table
           Folding canvas chair in conservatory
           Fallen leaves under tree and around breeze blocks

Off stage: Tray with 2 cups of tea, and sugar (**Anna**)
             Cup of tea (**Anna**)
             Binoculars (**Graham**)

SCENE 2

Strike: Draughts game
           Cup and saucer and other tea things

Set: Empty cup and saucer below phone on chest

Handkerchief in phone receiver
Piece of paper by phone
Empty flower-pot on chest

Off stage: Brown paper parcel **(Leonard)**
Saucepan **(Graham)**
Old book **(Leonard)**
Paper bag, with dressing and bedroom slippers **(Joan)**

LIGHTING PLOT

Property fittings required: nil
A garden and conservatory. The same scene throughout

ACT I, SCENE 1. A spring day
To open: Effect of cool sunshine
Cue 1   **Graham:** ". . . I can tell you that . . ."   (Page 5)
            Increase light in conservatory

ACT I, SCENE 2. A summer afternoon
To open: Effect of warm sunshine
No cues

ACT II, SCENE 1. An evening in autumn
To open: Dusk in garden: conservatory illuminated by lights from
            house

Cue 2   **Leonard:** "Oh yes. With pleasure."   (Page 40)
            Slow fade from daylight to moonlight in garden

ACT II, SCENE 2. An autumn morning
To open: Effect of clear cold daylight
No cues

EFFECTS PLOT

ACT I

Scene 1

Scene 2

ACT II

Scene 1

Scene 2

Printed in Great Britain by Butler & Tanner Ltd, Frome and London